Together **WE** wheel!

BEYOND THE FINISH

A Story of Passion, Brotherhood,
and Relentless Determination

BRENT & KYLE PEASE
with Todd Civin

www.mascotbooks.com

BEYOND THE FINISH

A Story of Passion, Brotherhood, and Relentless Determination

For more information, please contact:
Mascot Books
620 Herndon Parkway #320
Herndon, VA 20170
info@mascotbooks.com

Library of Congress Control Number: 2019935687

CPSIA Code: PRFRE0419A
ISBN-13: 978-1-64307-398-9

Printed in Canada

To Mom and Dad, the first coaches we ever had.
To Evan, our everlasting teammate and brother.
We love and thank you all endlessly.

CONTENTS

INTRODUCTION

Prior to today, my timeline of life has been dotted with some unforgettable moments. If I had to tally them into a top ten, I believe that the list would include my graduation from high school, the weddings of my brothers, my entry into and graduation from college, the birth of my niece Caroline and my nephew Henry, completing the New York City Marathon, and my relationship with my church.

Prior to today, I am sure that my list would include the crossing of many finish lines, the beginning of our foundation only a few short years ago, and the many smiles we've witnessed on the faces of athletes, family and friends, as those KPF athletes competed in and succeeded in another race.

Prior to today, among my greatest life experiences have been breaking the barrier in the Peachtree Road Race and, of course, breaking the tape at IRONMAN Wisconsin and IRONMAN Florida and hearing the announcer bellow, "Brent Pease...Kyle Pease...You are an IRONMAN."

But then today came. And as wonderful as each of those life-affecting moments were, they have been temporarily dwarfed by the magnitude of today.

You see, today, just moments ago, Brent and I crossed the finish line TOGETHER at IRONMAN 70.3 in Raleigh, North Carolina. And that word, TOGETHER, needs to be capitalized. An official from IRONMAN approached us shortly after we crossed the finish line and announced, "Brent and Kyle, as you know, it's the fortieth anniversary, and we want you to inspire us for the next forty years. So, on behalf of IRONMAN, you're going to Kona."

Together, we trembled as we heard the unreal words leave his lips. Together, we were sure that we were dreaming. Together, we cried as we heard his powerful words. Together, we are still battling to catch our collective breath as we process this incredible news. Together.

This is a dream come true. Who would have ever imagined that a man who has never taken a step under his own power would be blessed with the opportunity to compete with the world's greatest athletes in the Super Bowl of IRONMAN at Kona, Hawaii? The only thing more incredible than this is that I'll be able to experience it with my best friend, my brother, my arms and legs, Brent.

KONA will undoubtedly test our mental and physical abilities, but to be out there for 140.6 miles on the famous lava fields of Hawaii with the greatest athletes in the world is the biggest honor, and Brent and I simply can't wait to tackle it.

Several years ago, we didn't even have a running chair; now we get to compete among the best. This points to the pinnacle of achievement and the reward for all of our hard work. And yet, this is when all of our hard work begins. I can promise our friends and fans, our family and our foundation that we will work harder than ever to make the best out of this opportunity.

KONA does not back down, and neither can we. These words have never sounded more incredible: "TOGETHER, WE WHEEL."

~ Kyle Pease

CHAPTER 1

AND THEN THERE WERE THREE

KYLE

"We all have obstacles. Are you going to let your obstacle define you? Or are you going to tackle that obstacle head on?"

- KYLE PEASE

If you think about it realistically, a guy like me has no business even being here. I was born with the inability to move my arms or legs under my own control. I need to inconvenience a hired aide or a family member to feed me each meal of the day and to bring my straw to my mouth just to allow me to sip a drink of water. I am unable to eliminate from my body or bathe myself without experiencing the indignity of having someone help me disrobe and wash my personal areas. My body certainly doesn't resemble that of a world champion athlete, but instead is cruelly twisted and contorted into the shape of a pretzel. And yet, because of the love and support of my brother Brent, due to our hard work and dedication, and through our relentless refusal to accept no for an answer, time and time again, here we are. Our journey began *innocently enough eight years ago, with a question shrouded in curiosity: "Hey Brent. Can people in wheelchairs do IRONMAN?" My brother's confident and affirmative response was the impetus to all of this. Despite many challenges along the way and several periods of doubting whether or not we would ever be recognized for our efforts, here we are: Kona, Hawaii, for the IRONMAN World Championships.*

O ur official first chapter began to take shape in the year 1985, when the world was quite a bit different than it is today. In an ironic case of political foreshadowing, America had a Hollywood star in the White House, actor-turned-president Ronald Reagan. Soft drink giant Coca-Cola, based in our home town of Atlanta, felt the world was lacking taste, and introduced New Coke to the market. (They abandoned the carbonated horror show less than three months later, apparently deciding that the world was perfectly content with its current taste.) A virtual unknown by the name of Oprah Winfrey made her cinematic debut in the movie *The Color Purple*, along with another relative no-name, Whoopi Goldberg. Perhaps you've since heard of them? An all-too-familiar scenario occurred in the Atlanta sports scene, as my favorite teams, the Braves, Falcons, and Hawks, all finished with losing records yet again. My current favorite NFL player, Falcons quarterback Matt Ryan, was not yet throwing spirals, but was instead making his entry into the world, just four months after I did. Of far more importance, at least in my life, was the fact that Syracuse University sweethearts Janis and Richard Pease were about to bring children numbers two and three into the world in the form of identical boy twins. Evan and I, my ever-so-slightly older brother, would soon join our big brother, two-year old Brent. Our Atlanta-based quintet would become known around our neighborhood as the Pease family.

Though I clearly played a cameo role with a front row seat to the main event, much of what I know about our birth, which took place on the morning of February 19, 1985, came via stories that have been passed down from Mom and Dad and narrated to us word-for-word countless times over the years. It feels as though the story of our birth was told and retold more often than our nightly bedtime reading of *Goodnight Moon*. It may be that I often begged my parents to retell the tale in order to acquire the details behind how I became a spastic quadriplegic with cerebral palsy. Though I've learned to live a very full and happy life despite my disability and have never known things any other way, it has admittedly had a rather large effect on my life. To be remotely unaware of the intricate details that had such a profound impact on me would be ignoring the rather substantial elephant in the room.

Knowing Mom as well as I do, I have no doubt that both she and Dad did everything that young parents were supposed to do during pregnancy—by the book, with little or no variation from what Dr. Spock or any other expert told them to do. Mom and Dad were young and excited to bring, not one, but two, children into the world. Following an uneventful pregnancy and the successful birth of our older brother Brent two years earlier, there was no reason to anticipate that this birth experience would have any complications.

Mom and Dad learned that they were having twins during a scheduled visit to the Ob-Gyn earlier in the pregnancy. The young nurse performing the ultrasound smeared the ECG jelly on Mom's belly and immediately held up two fingers. Dad humorously thought she was making a play on words with our last name, Pease, and inquired, "What's that? A 'peace' sign?" The nurse laughed and said, "No, Mr. Pease. There are two in there." Mom spontaneously erupted into tears. The nurse then said, "Hold on, I have to move this around a bit, because sometimes there is a third one hiding." That's when Dad almost erupted into tears as well. As history would go on to show, there were only two of us, thank the Lord. I'm not sure that Mom, Dad, or the rest of the world would have managed quite as well had Mom given birth to triplets. They later learned via ultrasound that we would be identical twin boys.

Evan and I were delivered by a scheduled cesarean section due to the fact that doctors had identified earlier that one of us was breach. Rather than risk an unnecessarily difficult delivery, doctors decided that on Tuesday, February 19 (oddly enough, the same day Mickey Mouse was introduced to China), Mr. and Mrs. Pease would become parents once again. Though Mickey arrived right on time, we were both delivered three weeks premature. Although this did not seem to have any impact on my subsequent physical challenges.

During labor and delivery, things proceeded without any unexpected concerns. The delivery room doctor and his team brought me, Kyle Thomas, into the world nearly two minutes after extracting my older brother, Evan Daniel, from the warm confines we had shared together over the previous eight-plus months. Evan was therefore referred to as the middle child, though in this instance it could be debated whether or not there is truly a middle at all.

Dad was asked to play a critical role in the delivery room, with his primary tasks being to feed Mom a steady supply of tasty ice chips, to keep her at ease during the procedure, to mop the beads of perspiration from her forehead, and to coach her through the double delivery. Dad tends to be sort of a high-energy guy, so some may feel that the fact that he was put in charge of keeping Mom calm, cool, and collected was a bit of a physiological oxymoron. With fingers crossed and expectations high, Dad came through like a champion, however.

There was so much going on in the delivery room following our birth, including nurses talking about Apgar scores, snipping and tying of a set of umbilical cords, and rolling multiple babies out of the room in little incubator carts, that Dad failed to notice whether the birth itself had any unexpected complications. All three patients seemed to be doing just fine; we boys appeared to be happy and healthy, with ten fingers and ten toes, just as the blueprints had shown. At that point, there was no sign of any birth defects.

Dad remained in the delivery room with Mom while she was being stitched back up, and both he and Mom actually joked around with several members of the delivery team, including our Ob-Gyn, Dr. Mack MacFarlane. Interestingly enough, Dr. Mack was a twin as well, and coincidentally, there was also an anesthesiologist on the team who was yet a third twin. This made for some humorous maternity room banter that kept the mood light while Mom was being put back together.

Dad began to fantasize about the good times we would all have ahead of us. Like many new fathers, he was likely calculating how many more boys he'd need to bring into the world to make up a championship baseball or football team, while Mom was surely considering the more realistic logistics of how to feed, diaper, and pacify two newborn boys while simultaneously keeping a rather energetic two-year-old entertained and equally nourished.

The blissful new parents both wept joyfully as their original family of three had instantly blossomed to five. Dad kissed Mom on the forehead and told her that he loved her before exiting the room, feet barely in contact with the floor, to check on the bouncing duo of brothers down the hall. Evan and I were transported to the prenatal intensive care unit, which Dad assumed was normal protocol. Like US gymnast Mary Lou Retton the summer before in the Los Angeles Olympic Games, we both registered scores of perfect ten on our APGAR tests, which meant that at the one-minute mark, our appearances, pulses, grimaces, activity, and respiration seemed to indicate that all systems were go. This is a score that every new parent boasts about for years following the birth of their child and holds in the same high regard as a .400 batting average, a perfect passer rating, or a 4.0 GPA. Despite acing the Apgar, the medical staff was initially concerned that we were both slightly underweight. I tipped the scale at about six pounds, and Evan weighed in just under five pounds. Being twins, the lower weights were not overly surprising, but for precautionary reasons, they made the call to send us to the Intensive Care Unit (ICU).

Dad arrived at the ICU and peered through the glass window, as most new dads take great joy in doing. He'd planned to point, ogle and coo through the window at us for a bit and then bring us back to the arms of our eagerly awaiting mom. The pediatrician, who we'd known since prior to Brent's birth, suddenly intercepted Dad in the hallway. He had been in the delivery room throughout the birth, but now approached Dad with a look of concern on his face. Dressed in his white scrubs with a stethoscope draped around his neck, he advised Dad, "We have some problems, Richard." Dad glanced over the doctor's shoulder into the ICU and saw that there were two nurses rather frantically working on both of us. The doctor shared the unsettling news with Dad, "Evan is in respiratory distress, so we're going to put him in an oxygen tent. We're also going to take some blood from Kyle to give to Evan, as he is severely anemic." We both had drip lines feeding us intravenously and were hooked up to a series of monitors keeping track of our vital signs. This was a far cry from the Norman Rockwell-type scene that Dad had hoped to witness as he pushed his nose against the window.

Dad tried to remain calm, but felt a knot forming in the pit of his stomach. Witnessing his two newborns in peril was a bit unnerving. He took a few deep breaths and regained his composure, trying to convince himself that this was a normal occurrence and something that the medical staff had dealt with time and time again. At that point in time, it appeared to Dad that I was the healthier of the two, while Evan was in a bit of peril. Evan was having difficulty breathing and as a result wasn't getting enough oxygen in his bloodstream. Dad recalls, "The doctor didn't really tell me much more, or maybe I couldn't remember as everything became such a blur. All I know was that I wasn't allowed in the ICU to be with my boys. I wanted nothing more than to go back there to hold your hands and kiss you or to talk to the nurses to see how you were both doing. I accepted the fact that this was a situation I had no control over and needed to stay out of the way and let the experts do their jobs."

Dad took another deep inhale and hustled back to the recovery room to see how Mom was progressing. He gently shared what little information he had gathered about their new offspring. He didn't want to get her overly concerned, so he sugar-coated things a bit and advised her that we were in the ICU having some necessary bloodwork done. He told her Evan needed some extra oxygen and assured her there was nothing to worry about. Though shielding Mom slightly from the truth, Dad really had no reason to be alarmed at the time. He believed that this was a rather rudimentary procedure and had no idea himself that it was anything out of the ordinary.

Mom smiled gently then closed her eyes, understandably tired after bringing her two future athletes into the world. Dad decided to allow her to nap for a bit and headed back to our home in the Morningside section of Atlanta to gather a second wind. He pulled into the driveway, entered our temporarily quiet home, and paced around the living room for a few minutes to dispel his nervous energy. He turned the TV on and then off again after flipping through the channels and finding nothing that captured his attention. He headed upstairs to shower upon the realization that there was really nothing else he could do at that moment. He got freshened up pretty quickly, threw on some fresh clothes, and grabbed an overripe banana from the kitchen counter to provide him with a dose of nourishment. Already out of ideas to keep his mind occupied, he made his way back to Piedmont Hospital about an hour later.

With only about three miles between our house and the hospital, Dad let his mind wander as he made his way down Beverly Road and on to Peachtree Road. With Springsteen's "Pink Cadillac" blasting on the radio, Dad tapped out the beat on the steering wheel, having a difficult time containing his excitement over his two new sons. He envisioned himself returning to the hospital to find everyone snug as bugs. He suspected that by now his boys would be safely tucked into their new cribs, with their tiny bums pointing skyward and the names and footprints of Evan and Kyle pasted on little blue signs above their beds.

To his disappointment, Evan and I remained in ICU, while Mom was moved from maternity into a double room. The nurse entered the room to see how Mom was recovering and was met with a string of queries from both Mom and Dad. A couple hours had passed since we were delivered, and neither of them had been allowed to see or hold their new sons. They asked when they would be able to spend some time with Evan and me and were told they'd bring us down just as soon as they could. The nurse reassured them that everything was going to be fine, but that Evan was still in the oxygen tent and I was in a crib next to him. Though trying to be relaxed, Mom and Dad began to show a bit of concern about Evan's well-being, while at relative ease that I was doing just fine.

They later learned the likely explanation for the initial challenges Evan faced—in medical terms, it is what is known as a twin to twin transfusion syndrome. Evan and I were identical twins, which means that when we were conceived, the egg split down the middle and two separate sperm fertilized it. Obviously not yet named, I was dubbed Baby A and Evan Baby B. The umbilical cord with all the blood and nutrients went directly from Mom to me first, and then to Evan. In essence, Evan was getting my leftovers. Consequently, I was born as red as a beet, filled with more oxygen than I would ever need, while Evan was as white as a sheet due to oxygen deficiency. If Vegas was laying odds, the money would have been on me to be the healthier of the two and the alpha male.

The medical staff performed a blood transfusion, which took some time to complete. This consisted of taking blood out of me, spinning it down, giving Evan the red blood cells, and then putting the platelets back into me. It took about two hours to complete the procedure and resulted in a lot of little needle pricks for both of us. Evan was not removed from the oxygen tent for a few days. Eventually, we were both moved into incubators, and at last, everything seemed to be moving in the right direction.

It appeared that everything was progressing positively, but it is likely that something catastrophic occurred. There are several different theories as to what could have taken place that caused my cerebral palsy. I don't think we will ever know for sure, and the way I approach life is that the cause is not really relevant. Though something had seemingly taken place in my brain that caused a birth defect, neither the medical staff nor my parents were aware of the system malfunction at the time it likely occurred. It took place behind the scenes. Initially, there was no indication that anything had occurred at all. Whatever transpired flew quietly under the radar and didn't become evident until I began to mature.

Mom was released from the hospital a day or two after the delivery, while Evan and I were finally released and able to go home to 656 East Pelham Road about a week later to meet our big brother Brent. I've been told that everything was kind of chaotic with three kids under the age of two all in diapers. My parents were still concerned about Evan, since he was a little lighter and the skinnier of the two, but this was simply chalked up as two young parents being a bit nervous while attempting to get acclimated to the fact that their world had been turned on its ear. Overall, everything appeared to be good.

We had a very nice house in a beautiful neighborhood. The baby blue nursery was set up with everything in duplicate. The room was decorated with two cribs with two little mobiles hanging above our heads with the intent of keeping us entertained once our eyesight kicked in. The rest of the newborn ensemble contained two high chairs, a double stroller, and two car seats; basically two of everything. Mom and Dad went about their business of being new parents for the second time, while Brent got used to sharing his domain with his two little brothers. Mom and Dad made the decision that their beautiful little family was officially complete and there would be no additional Pease offspring to join the clan in the future.

Three or four months passed, and Mom and Dad noticed that I seemed sort of colicky. I was crying more than Evan and always seemed fussy. My parents noted they needed to hold me more often and I demanded constant attention. My crying was disconcerting and extremely nerve-wracking, according to my mildly wigged-out parents.

None of this behavior was overly alarming and certainly didn't make it readily apparent that I had suffered a major birth defect. There's a lot of guessing that goes on early in life because a baby isn't performing much physically and is primarily learning through body language. They learn love and show compassion from hugging and holding, but other than that, they are merely feeding, sleeping, crying, and eliminating, over and over again. Then the infant begins to roll over and learns how to get up on all fours to start to bear their weight. It was about that time that Mom and Dad noticed that I was not progressing as well as Evan. It was particularly apparent when I was lying on my back in the crib and the mobile was going around overhead. I was not swatting at it or grabbing it like a so-called "normal" baby should. Mom and Dad did some research before contacting Beth Salzman, a well-respected NICU physical therapist and expressed their concerns about what they had been observing.

Beth scheduled a visit to come over to the house to perform some assessments. She flipped me over on to my back and had me play with some little toys. She had Evan perform the same tasks, serving as a case study. Beth noted the difference between the two of us and initially described me as "developmentally delayed." As these sessions continued over the subsequent weeks and additional testing was performed, those words tragically turned from delayed to a diagnosis of "cerebral palsy." Though the magnitude of my condition was not immediately known, I was officially labeled as "differently abled."

CHAPTER 2

"Life Ain't Easy, Growing up Peasey"

Brent

"I choose to look at my life as a blessing—an opportunity to show the world that my disability is actually a gift, an ability with slight modifications."

- Kyle Pease

T hough I was only three years old, I recall feeling heartbroken about what our family experienced after Kyle and Evan came home. Mom and Dad did their best to make the most of a confusing and extremely taxing situation, but I sensed that something was wrong. I could tell that there were differences between my two little brothers. I seemed to grasp that older people might experience tragedies, but I couldn't understand how something so "tragic" could happen to my brother, a child so young, pure, and innocent. What could he have possibly done to deserve this?

I know it seems like revisionist history that a three-year-old could sense that something was amiss, but that's my story and I'm sticking to it. Perhaps my brothers told me, in the secret language that kids (especially brothers) share.

Aside from those early feelings of concern, most of my childhood memories are extremely positive. Kyle and Evan were wonderful little brothers and a joy to have around. At first, of course, they were mostly just dirtying diapers and sleeping hours on end, but I remember vividly how my world came to life when they became old enough to appreciate. Having a couple of crawling, walking, running guys around the house to play with had been long-awaited and was well-received.

I'd say that the phrase "never a dull moment" could have been used as our family motto. We filled our days with the type of mischief three young boys are expected to get into. We played from seven in the morning until bedtime, wrestling, roughhousing, and driving our parents crazy.

Inside the walls of our home, we absolutely connected, but it took an adjustment to feel typical whenever our family was out and about in the big world outside our home. People often are uncomfortable and stare at situations they are not accustomed to seeing. Although the constant curiosity probably wasn't fueled by any malice or bad intentions, it was unsettling at first to feel like strangers saw us as some type of circus sideshow.

We created a childhood of inclusion and adaptation. Evan and I could have been encouraged to treat Kyle differently because of his disability. We could have handled him with kid gloves, marked him "Fragile," like a fine vase or one of Grandma's precious heirlooms.

But we didn't. Kyle was tossed, wrestled, tumbled, turned upside down and inside out, and roughhoused the same way that Evan and I played with each other. He was treated more like a crash test dummy or one half of the WWE Tag Team champions than like damaged goods. As you can imagine, Kyle wouldn't have wanted it any other way.

Our neighborhood of Morningside, an in-town neighborhood in Atlanta, Georgia, was made up of about 3,500 households. We lived in a two-story house with a gold brick facade and a solid black front door. It was not Mom and Dad's first house as a married couple, but it was our first official home as a complete family. After growing out of cribs, Evan and Kyle shared a small room adorned fittingly with twin beds, while I graduated into a room all my own, with a set of bunk beds used for occasional sleepovers. Though the rooms were relatively small, they were filled to the rafters with more sports memorabilia than Cooperstown and Canton combined.

Our bathroom was miniscule. The walls were covered in ugly white and red wallpaper with blue tugboats all over. We were young, so it did the trick, but the decor would certainly never be considered for a feature in *Better Homes and Gardens*. We were all born with competitive natures and we loved to watch *Double Dare* on Nickelodeon, so we made up our own Pease-style bathtub version. Minus game show host Mark Summers (who obviously wouldn't have been welcome in our little tub), we'd create clues and dive underwater to search for them. Kyle could hold his breath for quite a long time, but he'd often end up choking on a mouthful of bubbles from our Mr. Bubble soap, so we resorted to using other toys to fish the clues out of the water.

One of the more memorable stories in Pease lore was the time I carried Kyle down the twenty-seven steps which led from the second floor to the first so the three of us could play downstairs like "normal" brothers. My mom was horrified when she woke up and discovered that Kyle wasn't in his bed—until she heard the endless laughter downstairs. I think this was a turning point for Mom, as she accepted that we were relatively self-sufficient, even though we were young. She and Dad managed to sleep a bit more soundly each morning afterwards, knowing they didn't need to be at Kyle's beck and call at all times.

Evan, Kyle, and I were best friends and remain so to this day. We laughed and farted all the time (the latter a hobby we still enjoy immensely to this day). There are areas of life in which Kyle is extremely able-bodied, and flatulence happens to be one of them. We played for hours on end outside, games that we either invented or adapted.

We had a big back yard that was perfect for baseball, and when my parents ultimately added a basketball court, it was perfect for that, too.

Kyle was always included in some way when we played, whether as the umpire in baseball, or playing basketball with an alternative set of rules. We also built our own full-size train by tying together three plastic Little Tikes Cozy Coupes, in which I would pull Evan and Kyle around the driveway. In retrospect, this was the evolution of me pulling Kyle in the boat during the first leg of our triathlon journeys.

I think that my fondest memories, and most entertaining ones, were of us playing baseball in the backyard. Being good wholesome and proud Americans, we always removed our caps and started with a rousing rendition of the national anthem. We then proceeded to yell, "Play Ball," prior to the first pitch. If Kyle wasn't the umpire, my dad was usually helping him hit the ball and hustling Kyle in the wheelchair or in his arms to beat out every infield hit. We had lots of imaginary runners to facilitate the game, and the right-field fence was constructed like Fenway Park. As lefties, Evan and I both liked to try and crank one over the wall into Fenway's right-field stands. The laughter and occasional animated arguments were always a source of joy. That backyard was really where we brothers first began our love of sports.

When we weren't outside playing on our imaginary version of Fenway, we loved to sit in the living room and create baseball leagues on PlayStation. Dad created a modified joystick that he would wedge between Kyle's thumb and index finger—one of his first pieces of modified athletic equipment. These were the lengths that Mom and Dad would go to in order to ensure that Kyle was being included. Kyle's visual and observational skills really demonstrated his love of the game. He would tell us what plays to make or which players to put into the game, often serving as more of a coach than a participant. These skills are what make us such an effective team when we are out on the race course today. In many ways, I am still the player and Kyle is the manager, the coach, and the orchestrator, dictating what we are doing on the course to compete together as a symphony. Without this skill set, which Kyle is so blessed to have, we would not be nearly as successful as we have been.

We would also sit for hours in our bedrooms collecting and trading baseball cards. There was a baseball card shop by the name of Doc's just around the corner from the house. We went down there once a month after pooling our allowances to buy as many packs of cards as we could afford. We cleared enough space in our bedrooms to house a massive collection that we traded with each other every Saturday morning. Dale Murphy and Andre Dawson were Kyle's favorite players, and we could swindle some pretty one-sided trades with him if we were in possession of a prized Murphy or Dawson card. We all loved the Braves more than any other team and participated in many rock-scissors-paper battles in order to win the right to "be the Braves" whenever we played.

I remember the way Kyle's eyes lit up when he had his sights on acquiring a Ron Gant rookie card. He was one of Kyle's favorite players at the time and he would have spent his life savings to have that card. Today that card is valued at about thirty-three cents, so obviously his investment skills needed a little bit of work. We went on to meet Gant in person a few years ago as he did a story about the foundation on Fox 5 Atlanta television. I thought Kyle was going to jump out of his chair upon meeting his boyhood hero in person. Our obsession with collecting cards allowed us to learn the name of every player on every team, and this led to Kyle's love and passion for the sport. (Not to mention the gum that came with the cards was the best.)

Even though I felt like Kyle's protector, I didn't really have to worry about him once he entered grade school. He was not bullied in any way, and people always took care of him. My parents set the example, and it carried over to their friends and families, so he was rarely pushed around or bullied. I do recall one occasion that a bit of taunting took place. The words that exploded from my mom's mouth when she came to his defense would not be fit for printing in our relatively PG-rated book. Not surprisingly, it never happened again.

Our parents showered us all with lots of love, so even when one of them went somewhere with Kyle while I had to stay home, I didn't feel left out or lacking attention. My parents always figured out ways to include Kyle in everything we did. If that meant that they were the ones staying up late to host a party because other houses weren't accessible, then they did it with a smile. Early on, when Kyle was smaller, not having the motorized wheelchair wasn't as big a deal, but as he grew, it was important for him to be able to use it to get around wherever we went. That often posed problems maneuvering in and around less accessible homes, causing him to be excluded from events. It was disappointing to him, but he usually shrugged his shoulders and accepted the fact that he wouldn't always be included.

Evan and Kyle went to the same school for pre-K, but after that, Kyle attended school without him. This was Kyle's first opportunity to experience true independence. He didn't have his brother to look out for him, and he was on his own at that point. We found ways to hang out together after school and included Kyle in our activities whenever we could. He helped out my football team as we got older, and he always attended our sporting events, unfortunately often watching from the sidelines or beyond the fence. When he started playing wheelchair handball and basketball, they were often short a few kids, so Evan and I would come out of the stands and fill in. In these instances, we had to participate using wheelchairs, and learned a bit what life was like for Kyle. The difference, of course, was that we could stand up and walk away at the end of the game, and Kyle couldn't. He'll be the first to tell you however, that this is simply how he has always known life and that he has very few regrets or feelings of envy that we are able-bodied and he is not. It was fun to get the Pease trio out there competing together and perhaps foreshadowed what life would eventually become.

Going to Braves games together always stands out as some of our favorite moments as brothers. The Braves were just beginning to improve when we were kids, following many years of subpar, cellar-dwelling seasons. It was difficult to get behind a perennially losing team, but every April we had high hopes that this would be their year, and every year by about mid-June we were experiencing a hard dose of reality and waiting for another next year. I will never forget being at the game in 1991 when they clinched the division for the first time behind incredible seasons by Tom Glavine, John Smoltz, Steve Avery, Dave Justice, and our buddy, Ron Gant. I remember thinking to myself, *Wouldn't that be cool to do something like that together someday?* The feeling of winning together as a team was a dream, but one I never imagined possible. At that point, none of us seemed destined to be professional athletes, especially Kyle; it seemed as though that was just a boyhood fantasy with little hope of ever becoming a reality. How wrong we were.

Our interest in sports, and our innate competitive nature, may have a genetic connection. Mom was always in tremendous shape, running, swimming, and working out. Growing up, she was the fit one in the family, and she holds the title to this day. Dad was a cyclist and really enjoyed riding; his claim to fame was winning a one-mile bike race in Philly while wearing high-top Chuck Taylor All-Stars. (His shoe preferences, thankfully, were not passed down.) Known as "Downhill Dicky" among his cycling buddies, when I first got into the sport, he took me out to teach me a few things that he had learned along the way. He tried his best, but without Kyle's screams, I must admit, I am not one for screaming descents.

As we got older, challenges cropped up more frequently, but vacations were never altered to make things "easier" for us. We made trips to Rome, Canada, Yosemite, and many other places that may not seem like typical wheelchair-accessible vacation destinations. (To be fair, Toronto was extremely accessible as far back as the mid-nineties, as I recall.) The beach was a family favorite, and my dad or mom always brought Kyle out in the ocean with everyone else.

We traveled as a family to Kyle's physical therapy in California when we were young and stayed at the same Marriott hotel each time we visited. When Kyle and I travel to races now, it's like we are kids again—staying in hotels, living out of suitcases, and further solidifying our brotherly bond. We made friends with the cleaning staff at the hotel. They got us personalized Marriott name tags. As simple as that gesture may seem, it became a lasting memory for us. Sometimes, it's the little things in life that become everlasting, every precious moment leaving an indelible impression. It's a lesson that my entire family has not only learned, but has tried to teach throughout life. Pay attention to the tiny details. You never know the impact they may have on a person's day or future life.

A Few Words About Growing Up Peasey

Evan

Our family went to Yosemite National Park when Kyle and I were eight years old, and the trip has remained a favorite of mine ever since. It's a beautiful place; I'd never seen anything like it before, and it fostered a love for the outdoors that remains with me today.

I also learned a valuable life lesson about never giving up during that trip when we hiked to the top of Bridal Veil Falls with Kyle's wheelchair. My dad refused to stay at the bottom with Kyle while the rest of us made our way up to the summit, so we pushed Kyle's chair up over I don't know many steps and roots and up the mildly rocky terrain. Was it a dumb idea? Maybe. But the success we experienced, because we pushed hard for something we wanted and didn't let anything get in our way, has always stood out in my mind—especially since we did it together.

Brent, Kyle, and I were extremely close growing up. I think Brent and I felt an innate responsibility to look out for Kyle and to make sure he was doing everything we were doing. The three of us were all so close in age and had so many mutual interests that it was natural to share a strong bond. Sports always tied us together; playing sports together or watching our beloved Atlanta Braves was a ritual. While we may not be in the backyard anymore, that initial bond over sports remains today.

As a brother to Brent and Kyle I've had a front row seat to many of their athletic accomplishments: IRONMAN, marathons, and other races. Being their brother also allows for a completely unique perspective apart from anyone else, and while completing these endurance challenges is no easy feat, it's not what I am most struck by. To me, what is most inspiring is witnessing Brent and Kyle grow the foundation's mission of inclusivity, helping those with disabilities not only achieve athletic success, but also confidence off the race course.

My wife and I were in Kona to watch my brothers accomplish their dream, this insanely hard race that few people compete in and even fewer finish. I felt so much pride and joy. Those are simple words, but such deep, deep emotions that carry far more weight than I could ever fully describe. However, I'm most proud of Brent and Kyle for pursuing their passion together and I'm excited to watch them take the next step together.

CHAPTER 3

The Magic of Being Kyle's Mom

Janis

"Though I had plenty of friends growing up, I have to say that through it all, my very best friend was always my mother."

- Kyle Pease

Sometimes a mother just instinctively knows when things aren't quite right. I saw Kyle and Evan day in and day out as infants, and the differences between the two were quite evident to me. Friends who did not see them frequently might not have noticed the subtle differences in their development, but I just knew something was amiss.

I kept bringing the boys to the pediatrician, who diagnosed it as me being a hysterical mother trying to juggle three kids under the age of two. There were times when I thought he was going to prescribe something to me rather than to Kyle. When Kyle was finally diagnosed and my motherly suspicion was justified, I left the pediatrician saying, "I knew it." Though I'd steadfastly believed that there was some reason to be concerned about his development, I still couldn't imagine the magnitude of the diagnosis or the full extent of the challenges he'd face. I stayed positive and believed that one day he would outgrow his issues and be able to walk, run, and live life like any other child.

As the boys approached the age of nine months, Evan had some hernia issues. His testicles hadn't descended, and his stomach and groin area became very swollen. A pediatric urologist diagnosed it with a quick look, advised us that it was a relatively common occurrence in young boys, and scheduled Evan for surgery. A couple days later, while changing Kyle's diaper, I discovered that he was also swollen. We brought Kyle to the same urologist, who apologized for not realizing we had twins. He said, "I should've known. When one has it, the other has it, too." We later learned that needing hernia surgery is more common in twins born prematurely, so Evan and Kyle were certainly candidates. That was the first (and likely the simplest) of the many surgeries Kyle has undergone in his life. As Kyle got older, he also struggled with scoliosis in his back, which made him lean forward. That was remedied by having a steel rod inserted into his back during an excruciatingly long and emotionally painful twelve-hour surgery. Kyle was a strong kid and came through the operation a whole lot better than I did.

Our first pediatrician was a very good doctor for more common baby issues like sniffles, colds, and ear infections, but not so much for developmental issues. Beth continued to help and consult with us and proved to be invaluable, but we had a pediatrician who really couldn't help us beyond boo boos and bellyaches. It was decided that we needed a new pediatrician, one who could tend to Kyle's disabilities a bit better. We got a referral for Beth so insurance would pay for physical therapy sessions with her, and we were referred to an occupational therapist who would help with Kyle's fine motor skills.

We were also referred to a speech therapist, who got off on the wrong foot when he told us, "Well, if your son ever talks, and there's a chance he may not, he's always going to have great difficulty. You should get him a touch talker." A touch talker was a pretty archaic machine that had about twenty functions, keys that would say things like, "I need a drink," or "I need to go to the bathroom." It is a useful communication tool for those who do not possess the ability to speak, but we believed, rightly, that Kyle would be able to speak.

Richard nearly hit the roof and refused adamantly. "We do not need a touch talker. Let's focus on teaching him how to talk instead of encouraging him to not talk."

This was one of the decisions that made it clear how we were going to treat Kyle. Richard and I were in lockstep that we would raise him like any other child, that despite his limitations, we were not going to coddle him. We experienced many successes as a result of this "never quit" attitude and positive approach. For example, by the time Kyle was about three years old, he had pretty well mastered the English language. His speech was by no means perfect, as his tongue is spastic, but he was relatively understandable and did not lack the capability. With speech therapy, he learned to speak quite clearly.

Kyle was diagnosed as a spastic quadriplegic with cerebral palsy that impacted the use of his four limbs and many other functions. His limbs are not paralyzed, but they certainly have minds of their own. With the exception of some controlled movement in his right arm, he does not possess much ability to control his arms or legs. It doesn't affect his mental faculties at all. About two-thirds of those with cerebral palsy aren't as fortunate, but Kyle is very blessed. Many who have been diagnosed with CP do not have the ability to speak, struggle with violent and uncontrollable spasms, cannot control their head or limbs, and are impacted mentally. It's all about perspective, and Kyle refers to himself as one of the lucky ones. He sees his life through a glass that is not half full, but filled to the brim and overflowing.

It was difficult to find a preschool for kids with disabilities anywhere near us, but we were fortunate to find one about a half-hour away, at Temple Sinai in Sandy Springs. When the twins were ready to start school, I enrolled them there together. First and foremost, they are twins, and it is rather unsettling for any set of twins to be separated. It was quite obvious that Kyle would need more attention than could be provided by a mainstream school in those days, so it seemed more sensible to put Evan in a school that also taught children with disabilities. It was great for Kyle, since he got physical therapy and occupational therapy and he could see Evan in between. Inclusion there was very good; there were many children with disabilities of all kinds, but the kids were really intermingled.

We kept them there for a year, then decided to send them to a traditional preschool with an aide to assist Kyle. We felt that he needed a regular environment and the curriculum that a mainstream school could provide. Throughout his life, it was tough finding a group for him since, unlike Kyle, many students with physical impairments had intellectual disabilities as well.

Kyle attended elementary school at E Rivers, where Brent's wife Erica now teaches. Brent and Evan went to a different school, but it was being renovated, so it wasn't wheelchair accessible. In many ways, this was a blessing in disguise. At E Rivers, everybody was different. There were many kids from Section 8 housing, kids who were black or Latino, and kids from all different ethnic backgrounds. Maybe being different was part of the culture and really wasn't that different after all.

Kyle wasn't bullied or picked on for being different from the other kids at school. I honestly think that was because Kyle doesn't define himself as being disabled, but simply a whole human being who uses a chair for mobility. From a very young age, he was very outgoing and approachable and never played the role of the victim. He never portrayed himself as being weak, which may have made him a less likely target. His elementary school teachers were extremely inclusive and absolutely phenomenal.

There was a special classroom for the kids with physical disabilities, who were taught by both a special education teacher and an aide. Kyle had physical therapy sessions in the morning when the rest of the class was at gym, then he would return and learn math and reading with his class. When he entered middle school, we hired an aide specifically for him, as he needed more attention and was the only child in the school who used a wheelchair.

From the beginning, both Richard and I tried to live day by day with a lot of hope. We didn't spend a lot of time dwelling on it or wondering *what if.* We'd wake up and learn a bit more each day. We'd go to physical therapy, help Kyle to meet his goals, then go on to the next thing.

Richard and I balanced each other out pretty well. He was a really good dad and always stayed positive. When I was down, he was up. When I was up, he was also up. He helped me stay optimistic and refrain from getting sucked in by the reality of the diagnosis. We accepted the fact that life was going to be slightly different than we had envisioned for both Kyle and the family, but that didn't mean it was going to be bad—simply different.

As twins, I think Kyle's challenges impacted Evan to a degree. I explained to him, "I love you both just the same, but Kyle is just going to need more attention than you are." No matter how open-minded a little boy is, I understand that may be a heavy pill to swallow. I often wondered if Evan felt like an afterthought, and if he suffered because of that. Sometimes, I wonder if he still does.

Richard and I believe we made a difference, helping to shape our boys into the men that they are today. We kept things positive, maybe even to a fault. I was always a cheerleader and never let negative thoughts dominate our conversations for long. I often told them, if you're ever in a therapist's chair, just tell them that your mother did it to you.

Whether or not Kyle would ever walk was never really a concern; we'd get by, one way or the other. Kyle and I once had a conversation while we were in the car together. He said he thought it might have been better if he had experienced how it felt to walk and then lost that ability. I told him I thought it was easier this way—since he's never experienced it, he doesn't know what he's missing. It was fairly commonplace for Kyle and me to have conversations of this sort, yet I can honestly say we didn't dwell on it. We accepted his differences and literally and figuratively "rolled with it."

In the summertime, Kyle went to a very inclusive camp. He absolutely loved it, and he made a friend there who was very similar to him in attitude and abilities. They had each other over for sleepovers, which worked out well. Not everyone knows how to get a disabled child undressed, ready for bed, and then dressed again the next day, which made it difficult for Kyle to sleepover at other homes. Evan had friends who would occasionally include Kyle in events, but most of the parties took place at our house.

Of course, there were obvious physical differences between Kyle and other children, but I saw him as just needing a little bit more help. He was my son and I loved him as he was, with all his perfections and imperfections. Kyle's disability never prevented our family from doing the things we wanted to do or from participating in all the things that we would have. It simply encouraged us to be creative, to think a bit differently, and to find alternate ways to include him.

We figured out very early on that Kyle could do just about anything the other boys could do. It just required a bit of help and ingenuity. When we would go horseback riding, we simply had someone ride on the horse behind him to help support him, allowing him to have the same riding experience that we enjoyed rather than forcing him to look on from outside the corral. We also found an adaptive ski program in Breckenridge, Colorado. The boys would tether themselves to Kyle's toboggan and zip down the mountain together. Seeing the look of joy on Kyle's face and the way he would laugh while buzzing down the mountain eliminated any pain or feelings of sorrow that we may have had. That's what we always tried to focus on as a family, the simple pleasures, not the difficult times. That positive mindset set the stage for what the boys have accomplished today.

As a result of this inclusive philosophy, Kyle has been able to do many things throughout his life that he may not have experienced had we sheltered him. Kyle played baseball and soccer, climbed mountains, and traveled around the world. He went to public schools, graduated from college, and commutes independently around the city of Atlanta via bus and the MARTA system. As an adult, Kyle has worked several full-time jobs simultaneously, runs The Kyle Pease Foundation, and hires, trains, and manages his own staff of aides. The stage was set at a very young age that inclusion, rather than exclusion, would be our family motto.

I occasionally pondered why this happened to me and our family, but the answer is that we will never know. No matter how hard we hypothesize or believe we have stumbled upon the elusive answer, I'm quite confident that there is no answer. In the beginning, I was looking for a reason, someone or something to blame. Then I realized that we all have incredible challenges in our life. Some are more obvious than others, and it's just about how you cope with them in your own life. I didn't always think like that. I probably had a bit more of a victim mindset at first, but soon realized that I was not a victim, but instead the recipient of a wonderful blessing.

I've always disliked the phrase, "You are never given more than you can handle." We had a challenge and we handled it, but that doesn't mean that those people who aren't presented with this type of challenge wouldn't have been able to adapt, change, and handle it just as well. I'm not more special than other people simply because we were presented with a difficult situation and kept ourselves afloat. I firmly believe that anyone who is faced with a similar set of circumstances will always do the best they can and make the most of the life test that they have been handed.

Greatness has resulted from the things that occurred, in so many ways. Our sons have grown up to be such good people, who have the ability to see, teach, and accept differences in the world. The people that we have met, the places that we have gone, and the opportunities that I have found within myself to help other people with disabilities are all the result of Kyle's disabilities. I'm not sure that I would have ever found any of this had Kyle not been born with these challenges.

Baseball was always a passion for Kyle. One year at summer camp they scheduled a Braves Day, where the kids were invited to attend a game and tour the stadium. Kyle laid in bed for several nights, unable to sleep because he was so excited to attend. There was some bad weather predicted, though, and it was no one's fault except for Mother Nature when the whole thing got canceled the day before. Upon hearing of the cancellation, Kyle was absolutely devastated; the poor kid was in tears.

I wrote a message to the Braves the following day to let them know how disappointed and negatively impacted Kyle and the rest of the kids were. I didn't pull the disability card, but simply spoke to them as a mom and told them I hoped they would be able to reschedule.

To my absolute surprise and pleasure, the Braves actually responded and asked how they could make it up to the kids. They invited them to an upcoming game and offered to bring them out onto the field to "run" the bases and meet some of the players. The kids were ecstatic, I was a hero, and we are all Braves fans for life. It didn't hurt, of course, that it was the day they clinched their first pennant. It's a fond memory for our family to this day. That's just some of the magic of being Kyle's mom.

CHAPTER 4

SEEING THINGS DAD'S WAY

RICHARD

"It must have been extremely difficult but empowering to be my parents."

- KYLE PEASE

'm not really a what-if guy in any sense of the phrase. I'm a trained scientist, an engineer. I measure. I calculate. I compute. But when I analyze this situation, looking back to when Evan was in respiratory distress and put in an oxygen tent, I question whether we should have done the same for Kyle. Was he in need of more oxygen, too? Did he have a stroke? Is there anything we should have thought of that would have prevented Kyle's disability? We will never know for sure, but my hypothesis is that something along those lines likely occurred, and that the precautions probably should have been taken.

Whatever it was, Mother Nature took away some of Kyle's brain function. I was initially frustrated with the medical community, because I didn't need a neurologist to tell me he wasn't going to play professional football. But they felt the need to tell us that anyway.

What should've been this joyous event, six or nine months later, was now a tragedy. What does a parent do? It's like trying to make sense of the situation after your child has survived a car wreck or a bad accident—you just need to find a way to emotionally work through it. You have to go through the stages of anger, denial, and sorrow, before finally settling on acceptance. You have to live through all of that and eventually find a way to cope and move on. Janis and I did this at different rates and in dramatically different styles. Janis went and got some help and benefitted greatly from it. Maybe I should have gotten some help too, but I dealt with it in my own way. There was no book to be read which would provide us with all of the answers. (There probably were books, but none of them dealt with my family specifically.) For me, this felt personal, and I didn't need an expert to tell me how to feel.

We tried to be a normal family as best as we could. We didn't talk about it much. We didn't say, "We need to be normal," or openly admit that we weren't, but when you have a special child, you're just not. The whole family dynamic is not normal. We have spoken to many parents over the years who were at that same place we were in. They often felt devastated or stuck neck-deep in pity. They're good parents who want to get out of the spot they are in, but they don't know how, so they're stuck feeling defeated and overwhelmed every day.

Very early, we made the decision that we did not want to burden the boys with the responsibility of feeding Kyle or taking care of his needs. I realized that, as their father, I needed to be the one to get up out of bed and check on those things. I would be the one to get him up and bring him downstairs; Brent could walk down with us, and then they could start to play. I would bridge the gap. The story of Brent and Evan bringing Kyle down the twenty-seven steps is well-documented, but that was the exception, not the normal way that things happened in our home.

We played a lot of games in bed in the mornings to equalize the playing field for Kyle. There was a great video that The Kyle Pease Foundation used of the boys playing musical instruments, with Kyle playing the flute. He could get it into his spastic little hands, blow into it, and use it.

Evan was running around playing the trumpet, and Brent was playing the drums. They also became famous within the household, forming the first boy band ever. For reasons we won't embarrass them with, we fondly called them "A Band of Three Little Naked Musicians." They obviously never made it big, just boys being boys of three or four years old.

I realized I had to get up every morning without any expectations of doing my own thing; if I expected to mow the lawn or go play golf that day, it just wasn't likely to happen. I needed to be there for Kyle and for all the kids. It was really pretty intense. The most normal part was having three kids in diapers at the same time. The less than normal thing was that one of those kids had to be picked up more often and transferred into his wheelchair. As parents, that was just extra stuff that Janis and I needed to do, and we eventually did it without giving it a second thought.

We worried about Evan a lot because he became the forgotten little twin. While Kyle still needed to be picked up and carried, Evan started to walk and move around on his own. We tried not to take him for granted, but when you only had two hands and three kids, one of whom needed extraordinary amounts of attention, someone was going to be left out. Janis and I divided and conquered as best we could for all three boys.

Beth Salzman became a great friend and medical asset to our family, and she loved Kyle to death. She had been working with him for about a year, performing traditional physical therapy, and Kyle was making moderate progress, when Janis and I learned about a less traditional method of therapy called NeuroMovement. It deals not just with range of motion and strength of the bones, but involves the mind, to help you think and maybe develop alternative pathways around the injuries or disabilities. The more we heard about it, the more optimistic we became that Kyle would benefit from it.

We started looking for someone locally who practiced this type of therapy, but learned that there was no one in the Atlanta area studying or practicing it. There was a four-year program at Stanford University, however, and through that, we were able to find a very wonderful therapist in San Francisco.

We traveled to California and met an incredible woman by the name of Anat Baniel. She gave Kyle his introductory one-hour session during our initial visit to the West Coast. He wasn't referred to as a patient, but instead as a student of this therapy. I called it a "laying of the hands" session. Anat scolded me, but I likened it to that because it involved Kyle and his mind and body presence.

I learned Anat's story, which is quite interesting. She was born in Israel to a scientist father and a poet and garden architect mother. Anat attended grad school at Tel Aviv University to become a clinical psychologist. At the same time, she pursued her passion for dance. She worked as a psychologist for the Israeli Army for several years. While in graduate school, she began studying with Russian-born therapist Dr. Moshe Feldenkrais, and in 1977, she began working full time as a teacher in his method. She taught for Dr. Feldenkrais in his Tel Aviv institute and developed her own practice.

Anat moved to New York City in the early 1980s, where she quickly developed a practice working with babies and young children, musicians, athletes, and adults suffering back pain and injuries. She also began teaching seminars and professional training programs worldwide. She is renowned for her success working with small children and infants with developmental difficulties, helping them to achieve goals never thought possible by their medical professionals.

We were able to see Kyle physically perform so much more during these training sessions, because Anat would essentially remove his spasticity somehow and provide him with the ability to do more. The sessions were held in her house in Mill Valley, north of San Francisco, in a little yoga studio. We would be there for about an hour, with a twenty-minute discussion following. We found her to be very opinionated and extremely strong-willed. She let us know what we should be doing with Kyle outside of the sessions. Anat didn't have any kids of her own, but boy, did she know what was best for Kyle, and she let us know.

Kyle benefitted substantially by working with Anat. Unfortunately, we had to cease working with Beth Salzman, because we weren't able to do both types of therapy in conjunction. That just about broke Beth's heart. She just loved Kyle so much. We still see her today, however, and she's still a great friend to our family.

We flew out to San Francisco one week of every month for Kyle's therapy. We took off early on Monday morning and arrived in San Francisco around noon with the time difference, rented a car, and arrived at Anat's house by four to get a session in that evening. Then Tuesday, Wednesday, and Thursday, they would work together for an hour; on Friday morning, we'd get in a quick session before we dashed to the airport to get the noon flight home.

I would go one month, then Janis would go the next, one parent remaining home so the other boys wouldn't miss school. Occasionally, we would decide to take the whole family to the West Coast for the week. Since therapy was only one hour a day, we had the rest of the time to enjoy and entertain each other.

Anat became quite overbearing and difficult to deal with as she became nationally renowned. As the therapy became more accepted, the insurance recognized it as legitimate, but still refused to pay for it. Anat was charging about $200 a session back then, and we ultimately found that there were people popping up in Atlanta who performed the same type of therapy, saving us from having to travel, which was a godsend for us. We'd made the commitment to do whatever we needed to do in order to provide Kyle with the best care possible, and Janis could get free flights on Delta, but we'd needed to spend quite a bit of money while out there on hotels, rental cars, and living expenses.

We continued the therapy for many years here in Atlanta with a lovely woman named Terese, who also served as a nun. (She had given up some of her religious practice when she began to practice this therapy.) Kyle went to her for about six years, and it did a lot to help. It removed some of his spasticity, even though the release was just temporary. There was a period where he could walk with a walker a little bit, but it would take him so long to get anywhere that it frustrated him and didn't seem to be worth the effort. Eventually, he got to a point in his life where we gave it up.

We later tried other things, like an implant that went into Kyle's belly with a catheter that wrapped around his ribs. This device would pump baclofen directly to his spine. Baclofen is used to help relax certain muscles and helps to relieve spasms, cramping, and tightness. It does not cure these problems, but allows other treatment, such as physical therapy, to be more helpful.

We tried that for a few years, and it seemed to have a positive effect, at least on his lower extremities. Ultimately, though, the pump became a problem because of how skinny Kyle is. The pump, which is about the size of a hockey puck, started to protrude through his stomach and affect the skin. We moved it from his right side to his left side, but the same thing happened again. Kyle endured another two operations before we eventually decided to remove it.

Watching Kyle withdraw from the baclofen therapy was almost like watching an addict ween off heroin. We endured multiple days of him screaming, "FU, Dad," like he was a possessed horror movie character. Anyone who knows how even-keeled and mild-mannered Kyle is would have realized that this was not him speaking, but the elimination of the drug from his body.

The boy's favorite pastime seemed to be playing whatever game they could conjure up in the backyard. I would join them on the weekends, and it always started with the national anthem, as the boys mentioned. We eventually started a Thanksgiving Day football game that pitted Brent and Kyle against Evan and me, complete with uniforms and a "team car" to drop us off for the start of the game. Those were some amazing times with my boys and just what I had envisioned in the hospital all those years before. As one would expect, things did get a bit competitive at times, but when I watch Kyle competing in IRONMAN, I appreciate the intensity he always exhibited when he was included on the field of play. That's just some of the fun of being Kyle's dad.

CHAPTER 5

THE INSPIRATIONAL EXPERIENCE
OF GROWING UP PEASEY

KYLE

"Life doesn't always happen as you plan."

- KYLE PEASE

The day we left from Atlanta was high stress. We were in the parking lot of my condo and my wheelchair didn't want to cooperate. My dead-in-the-water wheelchair seemed devastating, as we were against a time crunch. We were able to contact our wheelchair mechanic, who rushed over and diagnosed and repaired the issue quite quickly.

This is symbolic of the way life can be for me at times. Even at my absolute peak, things can occur that may be non-issues for most people, but end up being a bit of a challenge for me.

After a long travel day that took us from Atlanta to L.A. and from L.A. to Kona, the plane touched down. There was a completely different vibe which engulfed Kona. You could feel the island mojo, and it was difficult not to get swept up by the emotion of the island.

Once we got to the hotel, I spent some time with my caregivers, Melissa and Anna, getting acclimated. We had adjoining rooms; I had my own, with Brent next door, and the caregivers in another. This made me feel like a rock star, as we normally share a room. Here I was, at the IRONMAN World Championships, on the biggest stage in all triathlon competition, and I was excited about having a king-size bed, room service, and a room all to myself.

During the period that I received my therapy in San Francisco, we traveled quite extensively as a family. The travel was challenging, as things weren't quite as accessible as they are today. Though there is still much room for improvement in our country and around the world, things have improved drastically over the years as we become more aware and accepting of people with disabilities.

During each trip to the West Coast, we would arrive at the gate prior to takeoff and a family member would have to carry me all the way from the jetway to my seat. We had to leave my motorized chair at home and could only take a manual wheelchair on the trip. We would check the manual chair at the gate, and the flight crew would have it ready for us when we landed three thousand miles later. Someone would then carry me back off the plane and to the chair and wheel me to our rental car, where I would be belted in and propped up with pillows so I didn't tip over. It wasn't uncommon for me to whack my head on an airplane seat while Dad attempted to carefully maneuver me down the aisle and off the plane. No matter how attentive he was, I was sure to arrive on the West Coast with a nice welt on my forehead.

Bad weather made me nervous whenever we flew. My mom started working for Delta Airlines in the 1970s, so I was used to the whole airport routine, but inclement weather made me extremely unsettled. Once on the flight, I'd befriend the pilot, which helped me relax during those overcast days when turbulence was expected. I would ask the pilot about the flight plans to reassure myself and help calm some of the butterflies.

Though I knew it would never come to fruition for obvious reasons, the view inside the cockpit while chatting with the flight crew allowed me to imagine myself as a pilot. There are things I know I will not be able to accomplish, but that will never stop me from dreaming about the possibilities. Subscribing to that philosophy has allowed me to achieve many things that I may not have ever attempted otherwise. Much like the people at Nike, my motto is "Just Do It."

My family always found ways to include me in nearly all activities. They made sure I wasn't left out and that my life and experiences were like other kids. One of my most special memories was dressing up for Halloween each year. I couldn't get up the stairs at most houses, so Evan would run ahead and explain to the homeowners that I was in a chair and absolutely loved candy. He would either return with more candy than anyone else would get from those houses, or the homeowners would be welcoming enough to come off their porch to hand me some candy directly. Without even knowing it, we were indirectly teaching inclusion at a very young age. My Halloween costumes usually had sports themes. One year we turned my wheelchair into a race car, and I was a race car driver. Another year, I abandoned the sports theme and dressed as a woman. It is obvious that I'll do whatever it takes to get those Skittles. Brent and I usually carry Skittles on the race course; he has them ready in case we find ourselves in need of a special treat.

The family took a vacation to Disney World when I was about nine years old. I absolutely loved the ET ride and both Thunder and Space Mountain. I also enjoyed a ride called Crash Test Dummies, where you would get into a car and drive through the extremes of hot and cold, left turns, right turns, and ups and downs. You would feel like you were speeding on highways and then stop really fast. I could have been the driver on that ride, since you were not really in control of the vehicle, but I chose the passenger seat, a role I was much more comfortable with. The last time I sat in the driver's seat of a car was when I was little. Dad would let me sit on his lap while we drove down our street. It was highly illegal and extremely dangerous, but a very fond memory of my childhood nevertheless.

I've also climbed Yosemite in my manual wheelchair when my dad would push me up the trails. We would often have complete strangers alter their solo climb to help us up the mountain one step at a time. It was not easy, but we made it, and it was another example of spreading inclusion through our unique family activities.

Not everything is accessible to me, and when a place truly wasn't set up in a manner that we could navigate or we couldn't find a safe way for me to participate, I would have to accept things as they were and hang back and watch. Someone would always sit with me, though, and we'd make the best of it.

Throughout my school-age years, I was the kid who brought people together. Everyone treated me extremely well and was always willing to lend a hand when I was in need. I was just a regular student with slight modifications. I even got in trouble every now and then. As crazy as it sounds, that made me feel wonderful, as it made it obvious that I was not being coddled or treated differently than others. You would think that would have been an opportunity for me to use my disability to my advantage, but just the opposite. I really wanted to be acknowledged for my successes and held accountable for my occasional poor judgment. My goal was and always will be to be viewed as Kyle, not as the disabled guy in the chair.

There were several other kids with disabilities in my school, but I was the only disabled student in my classroom. My second-grade teacher, Ms. Wamberg, would take me out of my wheelchair and set me on the ground with the other students when we were reading as a class. She made me feel like I was no different than the able-bodied children in my class.

During a school play one year, my classmates sang the song "Hero," by Mariah Carey, situated around me at the front of the stage. It seems kind of contrived as I think about it now, but it showed me that I can bring inspiration to others through my disability. Seeing me participate in mainstream classes and get a regular education, watching me ride the school bus, or hanging out with me on the playground allowed the other kids to get to know me and accept me. All too often, people are afraid of what they don't understand, and this fear leads to prejudice and exclusion. The more we encourage people to get to know the person inside the disabled body, the more the stigma and the feelings of uneasiness dissipate.

Though I had plenty of friends growing up, my most influential friend was my mother. She never took no for an answer, and that instilled a positive attitude and sense of determination in me. I knew she had my back and would always go to battle for me when needed. She was there for me whenever I would begin to wonder "why me," and her attitude helped bring my spirits back up.

I don't think I fully understood what I could achieve until I became a teenager; then the "why me" moments subsided. I still have bad days on occasion, when I question why I played the role of sacrificial lamb, and I certainly wish things were easier for me physically.

I often ponder what I would do if I could choose whether or not to have a disability. As odd as it may seem, I'd choose to have it. This is how I was born. I accept it as a blessing, and I don't know any other way. We all have obstacles that we are challenged to overcome; being born with a disability was mine. It made me a stronger person, and based on the role that I have taken on, my experiences help make other people stronger as well. Had I been born without a disability, my potential impact on others would likely not have been as great. That is a gift I have received, and I wouldn't choose to give it up in exchange for the ability to walk or talk without an impediment.

I sometimes sit and wonder why I was placed in this position. Sometimes the everyday challenges can get a bit overwhelming. In the end, I believe that there is a plan for all of us. The plan for me was to inspire, to show people that anything is truly possible and that we all have been given special gifts. Once we're able to identify our gifts and put them to use, we can become the people we were intended to be.

Perhaps I sacrificed the gift of mobility in exchange for the gift of inspiration. I have really embraced what my family has taught me about being strong and being a valuable member of society. Because of who I am, and in part because of my disability, I'm able to show people that there are no obstacles they can't overcome. My perseverance and positive spirit allow me to inspire them to see the same limitless capability in themselves.

Mom and Dad both loved sports and knew we loved them too, so they took us to Braves and Falcons games as often as they could. At home, we would play whiffle ball and make up rules that made it possible for me to play, too. My brothers would put the ball on the floor and then kick it to simulate a hit. Then they would run from the corner of the couch to the chair and back again—that counted as advancing the runner. Dad would try to make sense of the rules as he watched, or even sometimes tried to be involved, but he never really caught on. He just knew that we were laughing and bonding, and that's what he and Mom really cared about. It would usually be Brent versus Evan, while I was the catcher or the umpire, since I couldn't really run the bases.

When Brent was six, Dad was helping coach at the Northside Youth Organization (NYO) in North Atlanta. Evan was also about to start playing organized ball at the ripe age of four, but I had nowhere to go. We constantly had a blast playing sports at home, but there was no league for me.

Brent and Evan's Little League games were probably the biggest challenge for me to enjoy because I wanted to be out there so badly. The coaches would occasionally bring me out onto the field during warmups and allow me to shadow one of the players. Being included in the event, though not quite the same as playing, was the next best thing. When they were giving everyone on the team nicknames, I was dubbed "the Road Runner"—a nickname perhaps more fitting for me today, now that Brent and I race together.

My parents wanted to figure out something for me because they knew that I was hurting while I watched Brent and Evan suit up. There was not much in the Atlanta until Mom found a woman in the Peachtree area who was running a Challenger League. The Challenger League is a sanctioned Little League program out of Williamsport, Pennsylvania, that allows any child to participate, regardless of their disability. Mom and Dad went down to meet her; her story was exactly the same as ours. She was the mother of a child with disabilities just trying to give her child something to do. Mom and Dad watched one of their games and were extremely excited about what they saw. Their wheels were turning, and they saw this as an opportunity for not only me, but for other disabled kids in Atlanta.

Mom took charge of developing the league. She and Dad reached out to Beth Salzman and got her involved, and Mom and Beth got all the paperwork together from Williamsport and made a presentation to the NYO.

As open-minded and excited as the NYO said they were, they ultimately rejected it. It was a good ol' boys' group in charge, and they didn't want to allow a woman into their little tight-knit circle.

Unfortunately, they messed with the wrong couple. Dad stuck his non-pointer finger up at them and said, "See you, guys." My parents took Brent out of the league and approached the Buckhead League instead. There, Mom and Beth started over again.

The Buckhead League fully embraced Challenger, accepted it, and implemented it right away. The NYO and a few other leagues in town eventually got on board as well, once word got out and people started to talk. Mom, Beth, and Dad ultimately started four Challenger Leagues in the city of Atlanta at the same time. I was finally able to leave the bleachers and play the game I loved: baseball.

We only had a few other kids at the beginning, not enough to field a team, so they actually had to go out and recruit. It was decided that we would build one team for each of these leagues and then rotate around and play each other at our respective home fields. That's how it began.

Dad had to drive our wheelchair accessible van to the projects to pick up the underprivileged kids, who quite often had been born addicted to drugs. Many had parents in jail and were living in Section 8 housing with grandparents who often had no transportation. He would pick them all up, drive them to the park, and then bring them back home after the games. As you can imagine, they had little fan support and certainly no one to help them out at the game.

Challenger uses the buddy system, where an able-bodied baseball player teams up with one of the Challenger athletes. This is their service project for the league, which is a fantastic lesson to teach a twelve-year-old. The able-bodied kids teamed up with us, kids using wheelchairs or walkers, and help us hit the ball and run the bases. All games were played on a standard Little League field. No one kept score and everyone got to come to the plate each inning and hit. Everyone got to run the bases, usually all the way around, from home plate to home plate.

Now, I knew the game. I knew the rules and I was very competitive. I wasn't going to have any of that. I know if you get a hit, you run to first, and if the guy threw the ball before you got there, you were out. It took a little time to get me to accept the fact that I was going to be given a free pass all the way around the bases. It was totally against the way I viewed the game, and though I knew we needed help to play the sport, I don't believe in free passes. In most cases, by the time I got to first base following a hit, the ball had already gotten there. I would turn my electric wheelchair and head towards the dugout because I was out, plain and simple. Dad would come over and remind me that the Challenger rules said I could stay there and run the bases. I would insist, "No, Dad, those aren't the rules." We would have this argument as father and son almost every week. All the other kids would run all the way around the bases without fail, but I wanted to play by the rules.

There is another league today for kids with disabilities that is more competitive, but it was not around back then. Perhaps that would have been better; I could have exhibited my stubborn independence and desire to be treated like able-bodied kids. Today, I fully understand it and embrace it, but in those days, I didn't see the big picture.

I really enjoyed having that outlet, and I ultimately found other wheelchair sports to participate in, including wheelchair soccer and wheelchair basketball. Wheelchair basketball was fun because Brent and Evan could put the ball in my lap and allow me to run the fast break. I would hit the joystick on my chair and move very fast toward the net. The net was a hockey goal on the floor and the kids would throw the ball into the net to score against a goalie.

In those days, similar to the Challenger League story, there weren't enough kids to field a team. So, if they had extra wheelchairs in the closet, Evan and Brent would jump in to play and fill out a team. In many ways, all these leagues are the predecessors to what would ultimately become The Kyle Pease Foundation.

The rules ultimately changed to become more challenging; we had to dribble every five seconds, or we'd get called for traveling. As a quadriplegic, I could not do that.

During one of the early years of wheelchair basketball, Evan and Brent figured out ways for me to circumvent my inability to dribble. They would dribble, push and coast, dribble, push and coast in their manual wheelchairs, and I would follow closely in my motorized chair. As they got to the end of the court, they would put the ball in my lap, and yell, "Go." I would fast break, as fast as I could, for four seconds then put my joystick in reverse. The ball would roll off my lap and into the net. Everyone joked that I got the first unassisted hockey goal in wheelchair basketball history. Dad went out and got a trophy engraved for me to commemorate that moment.

In the early 1990s, I was also doing therapeutic horseback riding. Mom and Dad would take us to the horse park at Chastain Park. Back in those days, it was made up of several rundown boarding stables where they would do an assistive riding program on Saturdays. It is still there today, but much better funded.

I was their poster child at the time. The posters were professionally done, showing five-year-old me in my wheelchair, reaching my hand as high as I could with the horse's head coming down to lick my hand. Today, The Kyle Pease Foundation fully supports programs like those at Chastain Park, as we always try to remember our roots and support groups who supported us during the early years.

Selecting an elementary school for me was very difficult. Mom and Dad found a preschool Evan and I attended together at a Jewish community center, located in a synagogue. Evan and I started in the same class, but the synagogue had an adaptive learning center. As my needs had grown, the next year they split us up, with Evan remaining in the classroom and me going to the adaptive learning center down the hall.

The next year they moved me to Cliff Valley, which was located in a church. At the time, I was able to sit up on my knees. They would take me out of my wheelchair, and I could kneel with my hands out for balance. During reading time, instead of sitting at our desks, the class would sit on the floor with me and bring the reading circle down to my level.

Part of my cerebral palsy involves the nerves that go into my spine and brain. This is where all the spasticity occurs, and it makes me unable to control my left arm. One memorable story was when we were sitting in a group reading a book. My left arm flew out and got stuck in the hair of the little girl sitting next to me. I had it in a death grip and was hurting her badly. She was screaming, and the teacher had no idea what to do because you can't just pry my hand open. They ultimately wriggled her hair from my hand and calmed the classroom down. I used to get upset by this, but that is just part of what makes me who I am. While racing, my hands often grab whatever we fly past. It doesn't bother me, as long as I am allowed to compete with everyone.

When I started at E Rivers, we had to do my first IEP, the individualized education plan required by law. At the end of August, around the time school was starting, Mom and Dad asked to meet with my teachers to set up the IEP. By mid-September, no one had returned their calls. Mom and Dad got a little frustrated and called the Georgia Advocacy Office, a charitable law firm that helps people with special needs. The school administrators got nervous because I did not get the services that I was legally entitled to receive. I became sort of famous because of this, an unsuspecting advocate for the disabled.

Mom and Dad went to meetings and discussed my needs, establishing what I could do, what kind of assistance I would require, and even how I went to the bathroom. The end result was that I attended most of my classes in a classroom with Special Ed professionals. During naptime, I could lie on the floor on a mat like all the other kids. At reading time, they had these awful adaptive chairs that looked like highchairs from the middle ages. They were really ugly and very restrictive, with all kinds of straps and seatbelts for safety. Mom and Dad asked them to get the kids out of their desks and bring them to me instead.

These conversations helped us to realize that teachers learned from me as much as I learned from them. Every year as Mom and Dad sat down to create the next IEP, it became more and more obvious that I was teaching the aides, the teachers, and the other students what it was like to work and play with a student who had disabilities. This was the first time many of them had been around someone like me, and it gave them a reason to look at things differently, to think differently. Even the student sitting next to me might have been wondering about that left hand of mine that flew all over the place and got stuck in little girls' hair. Maybe he'd think, "I can hold that hand while we're reading a book, and we can be friends." Kids could figure out the coolest ways to interact with me, and I was able to teach valuable lessons to those I encountered.

When I graduated from fifth grade, I needed to attend a more accessible middle school. I went to Inman Middle School, where I was paired with a fantastic aide. He understood that he shouldn't do everything for me, just get the book out and put it on the tray, or get crayons out for me. He would make me do as much as I could do with my right hand, which has quite a bit more mobility than my left. He would also help me with my testing because that was one of the things included in my IEP. Outside of what was required, he really made me work hard for what I needed. Brent does the same to me today when racing, as do most race officials. I am proud to have learned those valuable lessons, as so many kids do during those years.

At the time, Inman was a so-called "bussing" school, and they had a diverse population. The athletics programs started to grow and they formed an actual basketball team. I was selected to be the ball boy for the team. It was a very positive experience for me as well as them.

My next school was North Atlanta High School. It was a very famous high school in Atlanta, but it was also very big. Despite being located in Buckhead, a very white, Anglo-Saxon neighborhood with lots of money, the high school was predominantly black. (Most of the kids from the neighborhood went to private schools.) I was not just in the minority for my disability, but also for the color of my skin. In an effort to fit in, I made Mom start buying me Sean John and all the clothes the other kids were wearing. I also wore my pants really low, because that's what all the guys did. I became so accepted there that I was ultimately named the homecoming king. The homecoming queen, who was African American, walked down the aisle in her white dress with me, holding hands as best as we could. All the girls were screaming from the bleachers, "Kyle, we love you."

I later became the equipment manager for the girls' basketball team. In my senior year, the team went to the state championship game on a Saturday in Macon, Georgia. There is still a picture on the gymnasium wall of all the girls and me at that game. It would be my first real taste of competing at a high level. Even though my job was mostly to pass out the towels, the girls treated me as one of the team, and I felt like I was part of their ultimate success.

I had a canine assistant from Canine Companions while I was in elementary school, a golden retriever named Pete Kroger after one of the program sponsors. We trained together for a year to learn commands and what Pete could do for me. He became my friend and companion, but could also turn on lights, open doors, and pick things up that I dropped and put them back on the tray.

In 1996 during the Olympics, Kroger's was kind enough to invite Pete on a blimp ride over the city of Atlanta to enjoy the sites from high overhead, and Pete brought my family along as well. The weather was inclement during our first attempt, but we rescheduled, and it was an incredible experience. We traveled at a very low altitude, which allowed us to experience the sights like we had never seen before. We flew over our house, over Turner Field, and over the Georgia Dome. Every time I watch a big sporting event and they talk about the blimp sponsors, I get a little nostalgic and think about the experience that Pete and I had above the skyline of Atlanta.

Around this time, we were invited to appear on *The Rosie O'Donnell Show*. As the show began, we were in the wheelchair section, located in the back of the theatre. The music started playing, the crowd started cheering, and Pete began to howl. The crowd got quiet as Rosie started her monologue, but Pete continued to howl. Rosie stopped, totally forgetting that we were on the agenda for the day, and barked, "What is that?" Then she said, "Oh that's right, we have a special guest who has an assistive dog," but she was glaring at the producers. One of the producers came over to us and said the dog had to leave the studio. Rosie was very strict and didn't want Pete disrupting the show. It was initially supposed to be a family experience that we could enjoy together, but Dad had to leave to take Pete outside. About fifteen minutes later, the producer came out and said to Dad, "I think I can handle him and you can come back in and enjoy the show." It wasn't how we intended it, but it turned out to be a great experience, and Rosie was quite nice.

The more I developed my independence, the less I had to rely on Pete, so we gave him an early retirement from training, and he became our family dog. The older he got, the more scared he became of storms. He would crawl under my bed whenever it thundered. I didn't like bad weather either, so I understood Pete's fears. Pete lived with us for ten years before he got cancer. He went through two operations to try to remove it, but eventually we had to say goodbye to my good friend, Pete.

For the most part, my childhood was like anyone else's. I tried to get into trouble on occasion, but there were incredible experiences along the way: arguing on a baseball diamond, flying high above the Atlanta skyline, being part of a state championship basketball team. Never would you guess I spent my days confined to a wheelchair. Much of what I learned helped inform who I wanted to be when I grew up. Growing up Peasey was a blessing. It makes me proud of how I've grown and continue to grow to this day.

CHAPTER 6

Reckless Stories About My College Self

Brent

"There were many times when one of us would leave the table in tears; it was just brother stuff, but no one was spared."

- Brent Pease

A s the Pease brothers aged and allegedly matured, the time came for me to enter high school. My athletic gene kicked in, and I made the swim team. I also rode the bench on the football team, indirectly experiencing what Kyle must have felt watching a game from the sidelines. I wasn't a terrible athlete, but I certainly wasn't the first one picked either. Through hard work in the pool, however, I improved greatly and finished in the top ten at the Georgia state meet during my senior year. Our swim team earned the honor of runner-up in the state finals, and I had at least a hand in that success. I did some intramural swimming in college, but I rarely, if ever, practiced. I just showed up at the meets, swam my race, and then went out to tip back a few cold ones with friends.

I wouldn't classify myself as a troublemaker, but I wasn't a perfect angel by any means. My friends and I pushed the boundaries, but we never got too far out of hand. I rarely stayed out until all hours of the night, and if I caused trouble, I was lucky enough to avoid getting caught. High school was difficult for Kyle, as not many kids were willing to help him go out or get to parties, so there were many times when Evan and I would just stay in with him so we could all hang out together.

My parents instilled morals, values, and attitudes in us, which we refer to as "never say never." They were moderately protective, but they let us grow up and learn things on our own. We were likely going to do things anyway, so it was better that they didn't feel the need to have control over every little thing we did or chose to attempt. We learned some things the hard way, but experienced many things we never would have attempted had they not given us enough rope to hang ourselves. All in all, our successes drastically outnumbered our failures, so their parenting method clearly worked.

After high school, I was accepted into and chose to attend college at Florida State University. This allowed me a new kind of freedom. I remember telling both my mom and my high school guidance counselor during my senior year that my only prerequisites when selecting a college were that I wanted a big school in the South with a good football team. Academics were secondary to me. Mom didn't think going to a notorious party school was a good idea, but I wanted to go somewhere and have fun. I didn't bring up the fact that both Mom and Dad graduated from Syracuse University, a notorious party school to this day. Apparently, the apple didn't fall far from the tree, though knowing the two of them, Dad likely did a bit more partying than Mom.

True to the Florida State reputation and not wanting to let my fellow Seminoles down, I'd drink myself into a stupor about six nights a week. I majored in political science, a degree I knew I'd never use. My grades were terrible. I was a B student in high school, and dropped only a couple grades down to Ds and Fs when I got to college. Though not a threat to surpass Blutarski's 0.0 GPA honors, I was barely getting by academically. I had to work extremely hard one semester just so they wouldn't send me home.

We drank, we partied, and we got in trouble. The unfortunate part of it all was that it was fun. I had no regrets or remorse, and if it wasn't for concern of getting kicked out which would have ended all the fun, I would have continued indefinitely. I did what I had to do to get by and my GPA was just high enough to remain enrolled. My primary focus was having a good time.

Kyle and Evan's relationship grew very strong while I was in college. They relied on each other a lot more and were closer as brothers. Without their big brother around to guide them down the wrong path, the two of them flourished and became as tight as I had ever seen them. Kyle came down to a couple football games in Tallahassee and we took him out to have some fun and experience a bit of FSU college life.

Evan, Kyle, and I still loved to hang out together, even during my party years. I got in a bit more "trouble" with Evan, but the three of us loved to go out and grab some wings and beers together.

I entered college thinking I had it all figured out. When I got my first F, I had the attitude, "Oh well, I'll fix it next time." Then I got the next one and thought, "Oh well, at least I'm having a good time." It was a very dangerous and destructive attitude, and I'm honestly not sure how I tumbled to those depths. I certainly had no reason to be rebellious, yet my behavior said otherwise.

Learning that triathlete, IRONMAN, and All-American boy Brent Pease was a drinker and a partier in college may be a shock to some, and it's worrisome how others will think of me after learning about my dark side. That's how I was in high school, always worried about how others perceived me. When I got to college, I cared less and less, and it was actually kind of liberating. I was able to enjoy myself and not worry so much about all the responsibilities that came with being the oldest son and the older brother. It took me the better part of three years to start to grow up.

Once I graduated from college (by the very skin of my teeth, I might add), I accepted the fact that I'd have to get an actual job and do adult things. I began my big boy career, not in politics, as my major should have prepared me for, but in real estate, and I was moderately successful early on for a kid my age. I was making decent money right off the bat, but I was blowing through it faster than I could earn it. A life of fast food, dinners out, and a continued enjoyment of alcohol caused me to put on weight, as I wasn't sixteen anymore or playing sports every day. I wasn't doing much of anything, as a matter of fact, except for working and partying. One night after work, I went for a run with a few guys. One of the guys I was running with wasn't in shape either, and he was really struggling. He pulled off the course and poured himself a glass of wine instead. Though I didn't join him, it was indicative of the lifestyle I was beginning to lead.

I was working for my dad in those days, learning the ropes of multi-family construction and project management. I felt the need to work extra hard to prove that I belonged, and often would be on a job site by 5:30 in the morning. My dad and I enjoyed working together and had several great years before the economy forced us to part ways vocationally. It may have turned out to be a bit of good luck, as I am not sure I would be where I am today had I not been forced to reassess my professional and personal life in those years.

I concluded that I wanted to do something more with my life. I was tired of spending all my money at the bar, waking up hung over, and feeling bad about what I was doing each night. I was feeling it in the morning at work, usually reeked of alcohol, and knew I needed to make some changes. I made the decision to channel my energy elsewhere.

Working those hours made the transition to early morning workouts somewhat tolerable. I ran my first 10K in 2007 with a handful of buddies and was pretty proud of myself for completing it. We could barely walk after the race, so we sat by the pool and drank beers until we couldn't see straight. That's apparently what a partier does after running a 10K. It was clear that I had a taste of the running bug, but it hadn't bitten me hard enough to dent my thick, slightly inebriated skull.

A year later, in 2008, I entered my first triathlon, and that's when it really set in. I could finally see the big picture and knew it was time to make a positive change in my life. I began to understand what mattered, and traded in my beer mug and shot glass for a nice, comfortable pair of running shoes. I actually started asking the runners in my group, "When's the next race? When's the next Half IRONMAN? When's the next IRONMAN?"

The highlight of 2007, and in reality, of my entire life, was meeting Erica. She entered the scene somewhere between the retirement of the old me and the reincarnation of the new one. We were magically connected and began sending messages back and forth. I floated the trial balloon out there to see if there was a mutual interest by telling her that a bunch of us were going out one Friday night. I wasn't man enough to ask her out directly, so I hid behind a group of friends and made it out to be just a casual, no-pressure get together. She and her friends were going out, too, so we figured we would all meet up. As Murphy's Law would have it, she walked into the bar while I was on top of a table, three sheets to the wind, or perhaps even four, throwing napkins for some ungodly reason. Safe to say she wasn't impressed by my antics, and I realized that the old Brent wasn't yet officially retired.

I went home and passed out before being awoken by the annoying ring of the phone. Nope, not Erica, but a buddy asking if I wanted to go out. Far be it from me to decline an opportunity to drink; I accepted. I looked down at the floor, and, with one eye barely open, spotted a pair of soiled khakis and a wrinkled polo rolled in a ball. I threw them on, inspected them for potentially embarrassing stains, and upon giving myself a thumb of approval, left the apartment and started drinking again. I came home that afternoon, fell asleep, woke up. Lather, rinse, repeat. The cycle continued.

Saturday evening rolled around. Erica had miraculously overlooked my initial indiscretion and agreed to go out. We messaged each other back and forth a few times to decide where we were going to meet up. I was a wee bit wobbly, since I'd been drinking all day, and my second impression was nearly as forgettable as my first, minus the napkin tossing.

Additionally, she saw me wearing the exact same outfit I was wearing the night before. I believe Erica left that evening thinking, *Fool me once, shame on you. Fool me twice, shame on me.*

For whatever reason, she decided to reach out to me a few months later, in the spring of 2008. By then, I had signed up for my first triathlon and I was trying to kind of change my ways. She gave me the opportunity for strike three when we celebrated with my friends after my first Olympic triathlon. She was thinking, *He's so cute, he's trying to get healthy.*

The relationship grew from there, but I was still struggling to let go of that old Brent. In 2009, I signed up for a Half IRONMAN which took place at the end of September. The following weekend I was back in Tallahassee for a football game, partying, drinking alcohol, out of my mind. I gained twenty pounds back and was basically doing the same stuff all over again.

Prior to that forgettable weekend, my all-time lowest point was when I got so drunk at the family Thanksgiving in 2008 that I "dropped trou" behind Kyle's wheelchair and started urinating on the patio in front of everyone. We were all drinking, but I was out of control. My grandfather wrote me a letter shortly after, telling me that a friend of his had almost burned the house down because he fell asleep drunk with a cigarette in his mouth, and that my life was heading in that ugly direction. He told me I needed to get it together.

In 2009, I really started trying to change my ways, or at least sort of trying, at first thinking, *Hey, I can do triathlons and still get drunk if I want to.*

By 2009, the economy had shifted, and I got a new job as a project manager looking after housing problems for homeowners. I made sure subcontractors were there to cut the grass, fix the rooves, and perform other menial tasks. It wasn't rocket science, it was low-stress and allowed me to earn some money without overexerting myself. It didn't pay much, so I supplemented my income by parking cars at night. And that is what a political science major from Florida State who graduates with a microscopic GPA does with his degree.

I learned about a Half IRONMAN that was coming up, but here I was, barely able to make ends meet despite working two jobs. I convinced my parents to front me the money so that I could enter and travel to the event. It was my new thing and I was all about it, so my parents were kind enough to oblige financially. They felt that I was at a turning point and were happy to support this habit over my previous vices. I supplemented their donation by taking what little money I had saved up and buying a bike, because that's an inarguably brilliant investment when you're trying to tread water parking cars. It was, however, the longest time I'd been sober since before I entered college, and obviously a step in the right direction.

The noose continued to tighten economically, and by the end of October, I was completely out of work. Sometimes things happen for a reason, as that couldn't have been more perfect. It gave me all the time I needed to train for and compete in my first triathlon.

I was captivated by the people who beat me and enthralled by all the training they'd committed to in order to become elite athletes. I was intrigued by the process that went into getting them to this level, and I was ready to commit to getting competitive with them. I was absolutely hooked, and I wanted more.

In many ways, my addiction to competition was not that different than my addiction to alcohol, only much healthier for me. This is not uncommon at all, as people with addictive personalities often trade one addiction for another. Whether a former alcoholic, drug addict, gambler, or overeater, it is not uncommon for triathletes to become addicted to the high that accompanies the competition.

I'd behaved in a similarly dependent manner in college, circling every Saturday on the calendar as game day. I'd been ultra-focused on having a good time, and had my party schedule mapped out in much the same way I create a training schedule today. I'd start partying on Thursday night and keep it going a bit more on Friday, but the real party took place on Saturday, when we'd tailgate and drink from wake-up time to pass-out time. I felt the same way prepping for triathlons. I invested several days getting myself primed for the big event on Saturday, only I felt so much healthier and alive after the new style of pregaming.

So, after my first 10k in 2007, a triathlon in 2008, and then my first Half IRONMAN in 2009, I didn't want to stop there. I signed up for my first full IRONMAN in Louisville, Kentucky. Each race I competed in gave me sort of a high, so I kept moving up on the ladder, challenging myself, and doing more and more.

I had the potential to be an extraordinary swimmer in high school and college. What I lacked in those days was a work ethic. Had I put as much time and effort into my training as I did into my partying, I would have been swimming at a level befitting of my talents. It was a lack of maturity that I struggled with, maturity I eventually developed. It is my strength as a swimmer which gives me an advantage as a triathlete, as I usually put some time in the bank with a strong swim leading off the triathlon. I look back now and I am glad that I didn't attempt an IRONMAN when I was younger. I wouldn't have been ready for a commitment like that and would have likely soured on the sport before giving it a real chance.

CHAPTER 7

"BRENT PEASE...YOU ARE AN IRON..."

BRENT

"It's a motivator for what has become our mission with the foundation and to grow that and get more athletes involved and have people know that there is so much they can do without placing a limit."

- BRENT PEASE

The months leading up to IRONMAN Louisville were a huge challenge for me. Having to part professional ways with my father, taking a pay cut, and taking extra jobs just to get by were only the tip of the iceberg. Relationships were strained and it was tough to keep my mental attitude positive. Despite all that, there was this goal I couldn't let slip through my fingers...the goal of becoming an IRONMAN.

I woke up on the morning of the race at 3:15, overflowing with excitement. My body felt like a hummingbird. I couldn't fall back to sleep, so I tossed and turned before giving up. I managed to squelch the flow of adrenaline and laid still in bed, thinking about the task that laid before me. This was a life changer in so many ways, as it was the realization of a dream. Overindulging and overweight Brent Pease would officially be laid to rest if I could manage to cross the finish line at the end of the day to hear the melodious phrase, "Brent Pease...You are an Iron..."

I stopped before thinking the sentence through to completion, as I wanted the first time I heard the words aloud to be live, following the completion of the race. Somehow it felt cheap if I dubbed myself an IRONMAN, though unofficially, before I had earned the title.

There were text messages waiting for me from Erica, which inspired me to a new level. There were messages from family and friends wishing me good luck prior to the race. I had received some cards prior to leaving for "Derby City," and I'd tossed them in my bag so I could read them as motivation before the race.

A bunch of us were sharing a house in Louisville, and I finally heard some bodies shuffling around down the hall. I used this as my cue to get out of bed and start moving towards the beginning of one of the biggest days of my life to that point. I rinsed off in the shower and shaved my face so I'd look good for the cameras. So much had changed from the days that I'd simply put on yesterday's pair of balled up chinos without concern for my appearance. I grabbed a Power Bar, some heartburn medicine, fish oil, and some vitamin C, and washed it all down with a Red Bull. *Breakfast of Champions,* I thought to myself before shoveling down a banana and a small bowl of cereal. I mixed up a bottle of Cytomax and water for a few extra calories and drank some electrolytes before making sure I had everything together for my special needs bag.

As we got in the car to head downtown, the pre-race jitters took over. The dynamic in the house had been awesome. The mood was light and I shared plenty of laughter just being around the other competitors. The camaraderie and light-heartedness of it all made it very difficult to get nervous, but as we drove to the race through a nearly silent downtown Louisville, the weight of the day finally started to set in. I listened to a little Widespread Panic and kept my mind at ease as best I could. I walked into T1 around 5:00 AM and dropped off my special needs bag and bottles before checking the location of my transition bags. I knew the volunteers would be there for me, but as a control freak on race day,

I needed to know where everything was positioned, just in case.

The rest of the Dynamo group gathered, and we walked together towards the water. I thought that the camaraderie would have calmed me a bit, but my nerves almost got the better of me. Concerns about the weather crept into my head, and a bout of anxiety found its way into my thoughts. I had to sneak away and walk by myself to prevent myself from flipping out completely.

Once we got to the swim start, I had an episode of sheer panic. Betty, Mikki, and Linda, three Dynamo teammates who were holding spots for us, couldn't get to the front since they were not athletes, and we were lagging a few minutes behind. It ended up not making much of a difference, but damn if I didn't almost lose it again. I was a bundle of nerves and just couldn't pull myself together. Much of IRONMAN is a mental game, and I was a basket case before the starting gun had sounded. I couldn't imagine what I'd be like mid-race if I couldn't get a grip before the damn thing started.

Once we had our spot, I calmed down a bit and my mood lightened. It was reassuring to have my teammates and my coach nearby, and I'd be hard-pressed to ever do another race without some friends nearby. As the hot air balloons lifted off and the national anthem played to mark the opening of the festivities, my heart filled with pride and started pounding through my chest. I looked down at my heart rate monitor; I was already at 150 before I had set foot into the waters behind Towhead Island.

My family showed up to see the start of the race. I gave everyone a wide-toothed, nervous grin, and quickly hugged Erica. Having her there to root me on was the realization of another dream come true. We had been through so much that year, and yet there she was to support me, despite it all. I needed to finish this for me, but also for her. She was willing to move forward with the new Brent, and was seeing the good that I knew was in me all along. It was time to convince her that the new and improved version was worth any struggles.

We inched forward in anticipation of the start and the cannon went off. My heart rate was approaching hummingbird again, reaching 160 as

I plunged into the water. I couldn't believe it; IRONMAN number one was underway. About halfway into the swim, my goggles were killing me; in my state of nervousness, I had pulled them too tight. I slowed down a bit and managed to loosen them, then did a breast stroke for a couple of minutes as I swam down the Ohio River. At that moment, I felt as though I couldn't even complete the swim. What a disappointment that would be, since I knew that the swim should be my strength. I got over the mental hurdle and hit a good stride through the finish at the wharf by Joe's Crab Shack. I had a goal time of anywhere between fifty-eight minutes and 1:05, and came in right at the tail end of the goal with a 1:05.

As the volunteers helped pull off my skin suit, I realized I was already fatigued. While I grabbed my bike, I remembered Coach Matthew Rose telling me to enjoy the day. When I heard the loud noise of the vuvuzela horns, I knew it was coming from none other than my personal cheering section, also known as my family. I gave them a thumbs up along with a big smile. Though they were likely nervous for me, they were managing to enjoy themselves, and I committed to do the same.

I pedaled the first few hundred feet and my legs were tight. I questioned how I could tough out 112 miles. Here I was, 2.4 miles into the swim and about 240 feet into the bike, and I was already doubting myself. To compound things further, I ran over the train tracks and my bottle of electrolytes went flying. I thought about stopping to pick it up, but riders were all around me, so I just kept my legs moving.

My legs began loosening up and my heart rate dropped to where it was supposed to be. I took a deep breath and settled into a nice relaxed pace. Matthew passed me and yelled out, "You having fun yet?" I didn't get a chance to yell back because he was already gone. At that moment, I realized I was having a blast. I was out on a 112-mile ride with 2500 of my best friends, and there was nothing but sun on my back.

As I turned towards the center of LaGrange, Kentucky, the crowd noise became audible. I saw a sea of green Dynamo shirts and biked towards them. My cadence picked up, as did my speed. The horns blared and Ernie, our team photographer, snapped some pictures as I passed by. I chuckled to myself, glad I had decided to shave.

When I turned down the straightaway to go back towards the LaGrange turn, I suddenly felt the sun. This was a long straight run, and the heat was beating down on me. I ignored it, along with and the feeling of fatigue, and pedaled through. My mind was winning this tug of war over my body and was helping to pull me over the line.

As I came towards the end of the second loop, the final water stop was somehow out of water. *You had one job,* I thought. *To serve the riders water, and you're out of it.* I grabbed some warm sports drink and got nervous again about making it to the finish. I thought about my mental state for the first time in a while and slowed my cadence down. I watched my heart rate and settled into a nice pace.

Then it happened, just I was about ready to hit the end of the bike ride. I cursed audibly and begged for it all to be over. I was hot, low on fluids, and didn't want to eat any more calories for the day.

I hit the transition and was off the bike. Even though my race plan had been executed to near perfection, and I was in just over seven hours, I was a mental mess. I hit the T2 tent and felt that I could never run the 26.2 miles ahead of me. My mind was screaming to stop. I was covered in sweat now that the wind wasn't in my face. The volunteers got fluids for me and helped get my running shoes on. I came out of T2 scared stiff, but not ready to cave in.

As I came up the steps, I heard those familiar cheers. I looked up, remembered to smile, and realized this was still fun. I could enjoy my "stroll" to the finish in about five hours and I would be fine. I hit the half mile mark, and there was my family. I began to tear up. I passed Erica, running close to her and squeezing her hand to let her know I was okay and happy to have her close by. She had been so amazing and was screaming her head off for me. My family looked on with pride and screamed as loud as they could.

As I left them behind me, I thought about all the support they had provided to me, and turned to smile one more time. When I twisted around, I caught a glance of Kyle's face, and he looked scared. I threw my thumb up to reassure him, smiled again, and turned the corner.

As I moved towards the bridge, I realized that I could do this. I grabbed a Coke at the first aid station for some instant sugar and energy. As part of my training and weight loss-regimen, I hadn't had a Coke since January, and it was one of the best tasting refreshments I've ever had.

I settled into a slow pace, one I was capable of holding for the duration. When I came back over the bridge, Evan was blaring the air horn and seemed to be beaming to watch me go after it. Evan always looked up to me, and he had no idea how much I looked up to him. To have him there with everyone else gave me that extra boost I needed as I ran toward the meat of the run.

I kept pouring ice down my shirt, fluids in my mouth, and doing one Gu per hour with food at aid stations as needed. At the mile eight aid station, another near-crisis occurred. I bumped into another runner while trying to get the top off my bottle and had to stop. I leaned to pick it up and couldn't do it. My legs seized. A volunteer came over and helped me pick it up, and I walked out of the aid station. I figured I could walk for a couple of minutes then I would get moving. I had no idea how I would finish, but I had come too far to quit.

I hit the final ten-kilometer mark and was home free now. My shoes felt heavy and my legs felt even heavier. I knew if I stopped moving, I was toast. I hit mile twenty-five and heard our friend and bike mechanic extraordinaire Allen Heaton yell, "Come on, IRONMAN." I smiled and made that final turn. I saw the finish off in the distance and picked up my pace. I had gotten lost in my thoughts around mile eighteen and had been in a trance, but now I saw the finish. Someone smacked my rear on the way into the chute. I laughed and turned it on, finishing with a time of 12:42:24.

Then I heard the most awesome sound of the whole day: "From Atlanta, Georgia, in his first IRONMAN...BRENT PEASE...YOU ARE AN IRONMAN..."

It was official. I had prevented myself from prematurely announcing myself as IRONMAN earlier in the day, but I could now repeat it to myself. *I am a freakin' IRONMAN.*

A volunteer grabbed my arm and my body went weak. I realized how tired I was. I had been running on adrenaline, lost for a few miles, but now it was all over. Emotions started to sweep over me, and I collapsed into a sitting position. Erica was behind me, beaming, and I had never hurt so good. All the long hard months, the sacrifices, the juggling acts. It was all over and it was amazing. I had never been on such a high before. This was something special. A volunteer asked if I wanted a picture with my medal and hat, and I nodded. I grabbed Erica and the emotions overcame me again. I cried in her arms and held on as long as I could. She squeezed me back, and I felt how much she had been there through it all. We had a bright future ahead of us, and I couldn't have been happier to have her there at the finish with me.

We found the family; everyone had tears streaming down their cheeks. I hugged my mom and held on just a bit longer. I grabbed Kyle and squeezed him hard enough so he knew how much he motivated me, and how much his support pushed me through it all. I wanted Kyle to know how good it felt, and hopefully that hug said everything that I couldn't at that moment. I grabbed my dad next, and we didn't have to say much. We had been through a lot, but it didn't matter. The love and support shined right on through and we embraced the moment.

To be an IRONMAN was so much more than the race. It shaped who I wanted to become and reminded me how awesome life can be when you commit. I'd started training in November and here I was, nearly ten months later, at the top of the mountain. I knew at some point I'd have to come down from the mountain and move forward, but I also knew that I could climb to the top many times over if I worked hard. Life itself is lots of ups and downs, similar to my race day. You learn to push through the low points and find the positive...one more mile, one more mile...and when you get out from those low spots, you reach a point that everything shines through. I didn't know what was next for me, but for today, I knew one thing; I was now an IRONMAN.

CHAPTER 8

CAN PEOPLE IN WHEELCHAIRS DO IRONMAN?

KYLE

"Today there are so many different ways people with disabilities can participate in athletics. If you want to do it, don't let anyone stop you."

- KYLE PEASE

While Brent was training for Louisville, I was curious about the logistics that went into the training and the execution on "game day." I became a student of the game, and I think this is what makes me such a valuable teammate now that we compete together. Brent is obviously the brawn, but I have become the brain and the heart of the Pease Brothers' race team. I put together the game plan and Brent executes it. As I think about it, it is not very different than the days we played Madden as children. I was the X's and O's guy on the sidelines while Evan and Brent played between the lines. The difference today is that I am the player-coach rather than simply managing from the bench.

I couldn't have been prouder watching Brent evolve as he became more and more involved in triathlons and ultimately in IRONMAN. I'm not sure that I was fully aware of his partying lifestyle prior to his evolution, but I had noticed that he was starting to gain a bit of weight and was kind of a disheveled mess more often than not. Seeing him get more involved in running was comforting to me, and I vowed to support him in every way that I could.

I knew IRONMAN Louisville was an event that I had to witness. I made plans with my best friend on the planet, Sam Harrison, to make the six-hour trek up Interstate 75 to watch Brent compete. That weekend gave me a lot of independence. I felt like a grown up for the first time. I got to book my own hotel room and do whatever Sam and I wanted to do. We got to live an adult life, drink beer, and hang out until two o'clock in the morning. I was so enthralled with my grown-up weekend that it didn't hit me until race day what IRONMAN was all about.

I had no idea what it was. I knew some of the basics, like you had to swim, bike, and run, but I had no clue the mental and physical toll that it entailed. I just really wanted Brent to be safe and not die.

It really and truly was a concern to me that my brother might die, and whether or not that fear was justified, it really had me rattled. I talked to Erica in the hotel room. She reassured me that it was okay to have these concerns, but asked that I not share my thoughts with Brent. I told her I would never do that, but that I was worried for his safety.

Though Brent had competed in several races of various lengths prior to Louisville, this was the first time I had seen him compete. Our brotherly bond really started growing stronger right before Louisville. He had always been my protector, throughout our entire life, and my fear was likely a bit selfish. I wanted to have the opportunity to play the role of the protector and to be there for him, just like he'd always been there for me.

The scariest part was that he was going to be out there all day, without any breaks, without any time to use the bathroom. I was trying to learn as much as I could, but my lack of true understanding of the sport itself and seeing someone put their body through hell were unnerving to me. Our bodies are not made for IRONMAN. Our bodies are made for doing some sort of exercise, taking a break, and then doing more exercise. They were never intended to be taxed and pushed to this length, without a break and to the point of exhaustion. As human beings who are addicted to the sport of IRONMAN, we ignore what our bodies are telling us and try to push the limit. That's the part I didn't understand about the sport, and that's what made me a bit apprehensive about watching Brent exhaust himself in what I saw as an unsafe way.

When the cannon went off to mark the start of the race, Sam and I had gone down to watch Brent take off on the swim. The start was a mass of bathing caps and flailing arms with splashing everywhere, so I never really spotted Brent going into the water. I'm glad I witnessed the start, because my apprehension was replaced by a sense of excitement, though I wasn't able to locate Brent as the swimmers hit the surf. I did see him once he was out of the water in the transition area where the swim ended and the bike leg began. There was a long set of stairs that came up from the river, which stopped me from going down to the water's edge to see Brent exit the water, so we felt the transition area would be the best spot to see him and offer words of encouragement. I was obviously not playing the same role I play today, but it was still important for me to give Brent my support and to make sure he knew that we were with him in spirit. This was perhaps when my wheels initially started turning, and I had an inkling that I would like to participate in the sport as well.

It was at this point that I really started getting to know Brent's friend, Betty Janelle. Betty, a former Division 1 swimmer and Kona qualifier, was there to support all the athletes that day. I was so into what was going on that I kept picking her brain and asking her questions. We went back and forth all day. With her big grin and loud, booming voice, she kept urging me to go do one with Brent. I wasn't sure if this was even possible, but Betty sure made me think it was. Betty, who has since become a dear friend of mine, has such an incredible spirit; it was hard not to get caught up in her excitement.

At one point, as we waited in LaGrange for Brent to come by, I began to get nervous. In the calmest voice I have ever heard from Betty, she simply told my mom and me that Brent was exactly where he was supposed to be. I took that to mean that he was clean, healthy, and living his best self, and not just that he was one of the last athletes in the group from Atlanta that day and had time to grow in the sport. No, Betty was right, Brent was exactly where he was supposed to be. Betty had my mind cranking about doing an IRONMAN.

My mind turned back to Brent once he exited the transition area on his bike. His bike, of course, also looked a lot different than it does today, as he was competing as a solo athlete and didn't need the heavy three-wheeler we now use to compete. Instead, he had a sleek looking, lightweight bike that allowed him to compete on a level playing field with the other athletes. He was not yet at the same level as many of the more seasoned triathletes, but that was due to lack of experience, not on account of his heavier equipment.

Once Brent took off on the bike, Sam and I got into the van and traveled to a spot about forty miles outside of Louisville so we could see him again, this time a bit before the halfway point on the ride. This wasn't by design, but turned out to be a good spot for us to pull over and see him, even if only for a few seconds as he buzzed by.

It's sort of funny being a spectator, because that's truly how it goes. You drive an hour or so and wait for several hours for your rider to go by. Though we root for each and every rider we see, our level of interest and enthusiasm in and for them is not nearly as feverish as when Brent pedals by. That is the commitment of the fan. We know that, as difficult as it may have been for us to wait to see Brent, our wait is nowhere near as challenging as the experience is for Brent. The least we can do as fans is cheer loudly, long and hard, and offer a bit of inspiration to get him through any mental challenge he may be fighting. Now that I ride with Brent, a big part of my role is offering him that inspiration throughout the race so that he doesn't have to wait alone for the next group of fans to motivate him.

Sam was extremely adept at scouting the race course via Google Maps, helping us catch Brent at several different points during the bike leg as well as the run. For Sam and me, it was sort of like a Thelma and Louise adventure, as we'd hop into the van, ride together, laugh and talk for forty or fifty miles, before hopping out and waiting for Brent to come by again.

Sam is one of my closest friends, and it is during days and trips like these that our friendship becomes even tighter. Prior to race day, Sam and I went to the Louisville Slugger Museum, which was another highlight for a baseball fanatic like me. The coolest part was seeing the bat that Atlanta Brave legend Hank Aaron used to hit his 700th home run. Aaron went on to hit 755, but he donated the bat that was responsible for number 700 to the Louisville museum. As a lifelong Braves fan, seeing that sent shivers up my spine and made me feel like I'd been there to experience that historic moment in baseball history. Since the event took place about fourteen years before I was born, that wouldn't have been possible, but it still was a heartwarming moment for a die-hard Braves fan. I also got to see Jason Heyward's bat, which was important to me. At the time, I was working at a local sports agency that represented Heyward, another Braves player. Seeing his bat was really cool. I took a bunch of photos and sent them back to the office to share with my fellow employees. Seeing how they made the bats and feeling so close to the sport of baseball was really exciting for me.

We saw Brent come in off the bike after completing the 112-mile course, cheering loudly as he prepared for the 26.2-mile run. By this time, Evan and my mother's sister, Aunt Susie, had joined us. We all hung out at mile one of the run. While we were waiting for Brent to cross in front of us, we all wrote inspiring messages in chalk on the roadway. I had Sam write, "Go Brent Go. You're almost there," which was not quite the truth, since he had twenty-five more miles ahead of him. Once again, it becomes mind over matter in an endurance event like this, so my words were well-intended if not entirely accurate. The hill at mile one was a curve right, which took Brent right towards the city. Sam pushed me in my chair for a ways as Brent ascended the hill, and I offered him words of admiration for as long as we could keep up with him. He gave me a thumbs up and a great big smile. He didn't say much, likely a bit winded, but the acknowledgement of the thumbs up and the smile made me feel like I was right there with him, participating on the course. I believed that, in some way, my words of encouragement would urge him towards the finish line if he struggled during the race. It still didn't cross my mind until after the race that this could become my role in future events.

Brent crossed the finish line in twelve hours, forty-two minutes and twenty-four seconds, and was announced as an IRONMAN in his first attempt. I had goosebumps seeing him finish the race. The crowd was so electric. It was exciting, being a part of something so special, not only for Brent, but for all the athletes who were giving it their all and pushing their bodies beyond the boundaries. Several athletes threw up as they crossed the finish line or were ushered into wheelchairs before being wheeled to the medical tent for fluids and nourishment. That's when I had the "aha moment" and said, "Wow. This is what I go through. This is my life." I must give it my all every single day, even to go to the bathroom. I need to have someone help feed me. I need help putting my bus pass on my arm so that I can travel around Atlanta. I'm dependent on someone else and these athletes are as well. They are dependent on their bodies to get them through, even when their bodies don't always want them to go through.

It was so exciting for me to imagine what must have been going through the minds of each finisher. They had dreams of becoming Ironmen and they were not willing to settle for less, even if it meant pushing their bodies beyond their intended limits. That's when it all hit me, watching finishers quite literally crawl to the finish line. Watching them fight their bodies with every mental fiber they had. I looked down at my own left arm, which was tightly strapped to my wheelchair as I fought spasms all over my body, and imagined what they too were feeling. They might have really struggled and been disappointed with their finish time. Yet the crowd saw them as Ironmen. They might have had flat tires on the bikes, or may have had diarrhea on the run, but nobody knew that. All the fans knew was that they crossed the finish line, and they were there to support them.

That's the moment that it all became clear to me, and I decided I needed to ask Brent if there was a way to include me. I knew I had to ask him if people in chairs could compete in IRONMAN, but I honestly didn't know what his answer was going to be. I knew Brent was going to be tired, and wasn't even sure if we were going to have a chance to talk after the race. I did know at some point, when the time seemed right, that I needed to ask him if there was a way to be included.

Brent got himself together after the race and we all went to dinner at a bar and grill in downtown Louisville. The name escapes me, but I'd like to visit it during a future trip to Louisville, since it is the location where our dream was hatched. While I waited on Brent to join us, Betty was back and figuratively pushing me towards my first start line. "Didn't you love it, Kyle? Don't you want to do this? Shoot yeah you can!" She was right. I needed to try this crazy IRONMAN thing. I just couldn't wait to talk to Brent.

I sat with Sam and Erica while Brent was with some of his Dynamo Multisport teammates who had also competed in and completed the race. I congratulated them all. After his teammates left, Brent came over and sat with us and continued wolfing down a long-awaited and much-deserved burger, while I enjoyed chicken fingers, fries, and some water, graciously fed to me by Sam, with an occasional assist from other family members. Sam, Erica, and my parents were around the table when I came over next to Brent and began peppering him with a barrage of questions. "How did it feel? What was your favorite part? What was the worst part?" He was very brief with his answers to me because it was ten at night and he was very tired. He didn't expand on them the way that I had hoped that he would. I didn't prod him further, as I didn't want him to get mad at me, but I had one more lingering question that I had to ask. It was gnawing at me, and I didn't have the patience or stamina to allow it to sit dormant until morning.

I looked him in the eye and asked him, "Could people in wheelchairs do IRONMANs?" Brent immediately responded, "Yes. Yes, they can." At that moment, our friend Betty walked by. Anyone who knows

Betty is aware that she is filled with exuberance, even after a 140.6-mile IRONMAN triathlon. She blurted out, "Hell yeah. People in wheelchairs can do IRONMAN," like only Betty can say. The light instantly went off for both of us. We had finally found a sport that we could compete in together on a relatively level playing field.

Prior to this fateful evening, we had heard the story of Dick and Rick Hoyt, a father and son from Massachusetts, widely considered to be the pioneers of the assisted running movement. Rick, the son, was born a non-verbal spastic quadriplegic with cerebral palsy after his umbilical cord wrapped around his neck during childbirth. The Hoyts began competing together in 1977 in a five-mile race in Springfield, Massachusetts. Following the event, Rick communicated to Dick, "Dad, when I'm running, it feels like I'm not disabled." This inspired the duo to continue racing, a passion they have shared for over forty years, competing in over 1200 athletic events and thirty Boston Marathons and becoming the only assisted duo in history to complete the IRONMAN World Championship in Kona, Hawaii. They also became the twenty-sixth and twenty-seventh members elected into the IRONMAN Hall of Fame in Kona. We had seen their story on television several years earlier, but nothing clicked with us, since neither Brent nor I were competing at that time.

Shortly after the dust settled following Louisville, I looked up the Hoyts on the internet and became inspired by what they were accomplishing over the better part of four decades. Their video, played to the song, "I Can Only Imagine" has been viewed over sixty million times, and I'd guess that about 500,000 of those were me. I watched their video repeatedly, mesmerized by their love and commitment to each other. The video brought tears to my eyes, witnessing the love they had for each other, their dedication to the sport, and their commitment to sharing the message of inclusion. Rick looked like he was really enjoying himself. I barely looked at Dick, but I was enthralled by the look of joy on Rick's face. Being non-verbal as well as a spastic quadriplegic with cerebral palsy, Rick may be considered to have more severe disabilities than I have. Yet, he was absolutely transformed from disabled to athlete through the physical efforts of his father. Watching them compete got me really excited. It allowed me to put the pieces together and began to lend credibility to my idea.

About six weeks passed, as Brent and I decided to allow him to recover physically from Louisville before we began to enact our plans to compete together. He asked me again if this was what I really wanted to do. I assured him that I was committed to this and had never wanted anything more in my entire life.

Brent reached out to the Hoyts directly to ask them for advice. One of the things I really admire about them is that, to this day, they respond to every email and every inquiry that they receive. They receive thousands of letters and emails a year, yet Dick and his office manager, Kathy, commit to responding to them all. They gave us a list of the equipment that they used and wished us good luck. Currently, only Brent has had the opportunity to meet Rick and Dick in person. I hope I can one day shake hands with both and thank them for helping pave the road to races like Kona for us.

CHAPTER 9

THEY WILL TELL YOU NO; YOU
WILL TELL THEM YES

BRENT

*"There's a red carpet there for a reason–to welcome
you. So you can go however you want to go."*

- KYLE PEASE

On Sunday, we did a dry run, which was our initial introduction to the island. It was a run into some tough headwinds which really had us nervous for race day. We were worried about both the winds and the temperatures, so that was playing on my mind. All in all, the week included a lot of rest and hydrating, and gave us time to focus on the biggest day of our athletic careers.

We had many events we had to attend for the IRONMAN Foundation. There was another set of brothers, the Aldrich brothers, from Boise, Idaho, whom IRONMAN brought to the race. Noah is only twelve, and his brother Lucas is ten. Lucas has lissencephaly, a rare genetic disorder impacting his ability to walk and to talk. Just like Brent and me, the two of them compete in triathlons. Just like the Hoyts were the pioneers many years ago, and served as the inspirations for Brent and me, we have served to inspire Noah and Lucas. Noah wrote IRONMAN a letter, advising them of their desire to attend Kona and to meet us in person. IRONMAN responded and got in touch with Brent and me. We surprised them with a trip to Kona, and also gifted them a new raft to use in their upcoming events. At the time, the brothers were using a blow-up raft that they had purchased from Target. Seeing how inspired they were by Brent and me also served to inspire us. They represent the next generation in what we hope will be a long line of successful assisted athletes.

Just to be mentioned with the Hoyts or the many champions that have competed and endured in the event is an absolute honor. To be part of that, to know that we've tackled the hardest one-day endurance challenge on the planet is beyond my wildest dreams. The Hoyts have paved the way for people like Brent and me. To be a part of that history is amazing. It really is an accomplishment and a credit to the love that Brent and I have for one another. Other teams have tried to duplicate what the Hoyts achieved at Kona, but were unsuccessful. Even the Hoyts themselves attempted Kona on three other occasions and did not finish.

There was a Nike ad that I found rather fitting for our journey. It said, "All your life you are told the things you cannot do. All your life they will say you're not good enough or strong enough or talented enough; they will say you're the wrong height or the wrong weight or the wrong type to play this or be this or achieve this. THEY WILL TELL YOU NO, a thousand times no, until all the noes become meaningless. All your life they will tell you no, quite firmly and very quickly. AND YOU WILL TELL THEM YES."

Kyle was invited to speak to a group of students at Woodward Academy, the school both Evan and I attended. Kyle read this quote aloud to the students and then explained to the wide-eyed group of onlookers how it applies to him. This, in a single powerful paragraph, summarizes Kyle's life. Kyle shared with the audience that we all have a disability in life. We all have something that we feel impedes us, or that we allow to hold us back. All his life, Kyle has told people YES. As Nike suggested, he has not accepted "no" as an answer and has attacked the world with an energy that is contagious. Tell Kyle that he can't ride independently through the streets of Atlanta on the MARTA, and he will show you that he can. Instruct Kyle that people with his type of disability can't successfully hold down a job, and he will hold down three. Point out to Kyle that spastic quadriplegics with cerebral palsy are not destined to be athletes, and Kyle will ask if people in wheelchairs can do IRONMAN. They will tell you no, a thousand times no, until all the noes become meaningless, and you will tell them yes.

Though we were in the infancy of our journey, this was Kyle's big opportunity to tell the world yes. He had probably told it "yeah" a few times, or given the world an affirmative nod of the head via many of the things he had previously accomplished, but our acceptance into the Charles Harris 10K in March was his first full-fledged YES. The world, which had kept him on the sidelines for the first twenty-six years of his life, had now allowed him to suit up and get into the game. We all know Kyle. Once welcomed onto the field, he was surely never going to be excluded again.

We threw Evan and Kyle a surprise birthday party as an excuse to unveil their new toy. It would be nearly impossible for anyone to tell Kyle no as he rolled up to the starting line in his sleek new adult jogger. Kyle tested his new wheels a few times during the following weeks before we decided to give it a test run at the Charles Harris 10K.

Skip, the race director, advised us that there was a time limit to finish the run, but we assured him we would finish well within the limit. We weren't sure if that would be the case, but we weren't going to allow Kyle to hear another no. We continue to include this race on our schedule to this day to acknowledge how and where our race career began.

Kyle showed up at the race dressed in his fluorescent green Publix grocery store uniform, as he had to get to work immediately following the event. With a smile on my face, I shook my head and asked him what he was doing in that getup. He informed me that he had to be at work by eleven. When I told him he was going to get sweaty, he innocently replied, "Oh, really? I had no idea." It was evident that neither of us really had much of an idea as to what to expect, but Kyle even less so than me.

In addition to his stylish Publix uniform, Dad found a unique way to add to Kyle's ensemble. Since Kyle has spasms and very little control of his left arm, it kept hitting the chair's hard side supports when going around some of the tough corners of the race. Being an engineer, Dad came up with a Rube Goldberg invention to prevent such a mishap. He went to his trunk and pulled a blue golf club cover off his driver and placed it over Kyle's hand like a mitten to protect his fingers from serious injury. This is another prime example of the adaptations we make in order to allow Kyle to proceed through life without being excluded. He also was supported by a blue pillow tucked behind his head for comfort. We were clearly the most unique looking entry in the race.

After the race, as we crossed the line after years of being told no, I asked Skip if we made the finish line cutoff. We had made it by more than thirteen minutes, and we both were hooked. Every year we go back to Charles Harris. Skip, the race director, is one of our favorites, and has continued to help advocate for racers like Kyle and the other athletes of KPeasey nation.

The first real big test for the racing brothers was the Georgia Publix Half Marathon. I spoke with the race director and explained what we wanted to do. I assured him that our safety, as well as that of the other athletes, was a big priority, and they had no issue at all allowing us to participate in the race. This was a far cry to the opposition that the Hoyts encountered in the late 1970s, when they were not allowed into many races and had to advocate tirelessly to be included. Our acceptance into the race indicates how far the sport has come. There are still many races that do not allow chairs or duo teams to participate, allegedly because of safety concerns. Like any group perceived as being new or different, there is often a sense of apprehension opening the doors. I always approach each race director to go over our race plan and ensure the safety of all those involved. This approach has opened many doors to races that might have initially been hesitant to allow us in if handled differently.

The Publix Half and several subsequent races included the three Pease Brothers, as Evan participated with us and took turns pushing Kyle. We originally began as three Pease in a pod, so to speak, before Evan moved to NYC and retired from competitive racing. He graciously handed the reins over to me and decided to become a member of the cheering squad. Evan and his wife, Emily, remain wonderful supporters from their home in New York, helping us through every mile with their love and support.

We arrived at the race site at about six that morning, believing that this would allow us plenty of time to prepare for our first Publix Half Marathon. Unfortunately, about 18,000 eager participants also had the same game plan. The starting area was an absolute madhouse even before the sun had officially risen. Somehow, we maneuvered our way through the crowd and to the front of the starting line. The music was blasting, the crowd was electric, and we were psyched to get started.

As the clock struck seven, the starting horn sounded, and we were off to the races. We were a little bit overeager to get out there and disregarded the game plan that our coach, Matthew Rose, had laid out for us. We flew through mile one at a much faster pace than planned. We were just so pumped to be running before the hometown crowd that we didn't heed his advice. The course got tougher as we continued and we paid the price for our overzealous pace at the start, but as we came past a group of our friends near the end of the race, the emotions were high, our knees started pumping, and our legs began moving more quickly.

As we approached the final sections of the course, the smiles got bigger. This was what we had been looking for. This was what excited us and showed what inclusion really looked like. We looked down at Kyle, and he was really fighting it too. The day had worn on his body. He was ready to finish, just like the rest of us.

We saw the final stretch of road and spotted the finish line just beyond our view point. Kyle extended his arms and let out an ear-piercing yell as we approached the finish gates. Anyone near us at that moment could sense the emotion and knew how amazing it was for us to cross that line as one. It was a dream come true, and at that point, was more than we had ever imagined. The support was amazing throughout the day. Everyone who passed us called out words of praise and encouragement for what we were attempting to do.

Competing in the race taught us two very important lessons, lessons that we learned through our experience and carry with us today. The first was to arrive early. As the saying goes, "The best laid plans of mice and men often go awry." Much of racing is not only the training and the execution on race day, but in the preparation. Prepare for the worst and hope for the best is the way we have learned to approach our efforts. We would much rather be early, prepared, and waiting for the starting horn, than scurrying around at the last minute, losing focus on the task at hand. We have also learned that it's difficult to do a race by yourself, but it's even more difficult to do one in unison. We had to learn to work together and to think about Kyle's needs. His body goes through the same type of stress as Evan's and mine during the race experience.

Kyle never wants it to be about him. Everybody who ran by us had something positive to say. He was usually the first one of us to respond. When someone wished us a good race, he said, "You too." He wants to live a normal life like the rest of us. That's why we're going out and racing. That's what Kyle wants to do. Anyone near us at moment we crossed the finish line knew how amazing it was for us to cross that line, as Kyle let out an almost inhuman shriek as we completed the race. The support was amazing throughout the day.

The finish area was a mob of supporters, all eager to congratulate Kyle. Though humble as always, Kyle was gobbling up the postrace attention. He suddenly remembered that he didn't want to be late for work, so we had to put an end to the party and haul him over to Publix. He had quickly come back to earth, tumbling from media heartthrob to greeter at a local Atlanta supermarket.

Earlier in the year, I'd gotten a call from Tri-Kids, Inc. in Atlanta.

They told us they wanted to help Kyle get to the starting line of his first triathlon. Tri-Kids, Inc. is a nonprofit organization providing training, equipment, and financial support to kids interested in competing in triathlons. The kids are selected from inner-city neighborhoods, and typically would not have these resources available to them. The program was developed to expose kids to a sport that requires commitment, dedication, and discipline, while stressing the importance of training as a team, yet competing as an individual, and how to apply those concepts in their daily lives.

Kyle and I were first introduced to Tri-Kids in 2009, when as a volunteer swim coach, I suggested that Kyle give the kids a motivational speech. Kyle was just getting started as a speaker at the time, and we thought it would be a great opportunity for Kyle as well the kids. The group was so moved by his story that before one of their triathlons that summer, they all scribbled his initials on their arms. Kyle attended, and following the race, remained in contact with the group, continuing to speak to them about racing, teamwork, and what it means to have a can-do attitude.

Towards the end of 2010, Tri-Kids realized they could give back what Kyle had given to so many with his time and effort—a chance to compete in a triathlon of his own. Kyle told the kids, "I know you might be afraid of the ocean, while I wish I could swim, bike, and run for you out there." From there, they helped set the wheels in motion for Kyle, and after a late December conversation at a Starbucks, it was settled that Kyle was going to compete with me at St Anthony's in May.

We heard about Curtis Cannon Henry, a brilliant bike mechanic. Curtis came to our house and he and Kyle looked through several catalogs in order to find a bike that would be a good fit. We were familiar with the type of bike the Hoyts used, but at the time, we didn't have the financial means to buy a $3,000 chair and a $12,000 bike. Fortunately, Freedom Concept agreed to let us use some of their equipment for our first six months as triathletes. Our first official racing chair was the Advanced Mobility jogging stroller, which we still use for athletes of the foundation today.

When it came time to decide on the boat, I discussed our needs with

John David "JD" Johnson, one of Kyle's professors from Kennesaw State. JD was an assistant professor with his PhD in human performance. He taught mainly sports management courses, as well as a general health and fitness class and outdoor recreation. He had seen videos of the Hoyts, and had noticed that Rick faced backwards in his boat while he and his dad swam. I wanted Kyle to be able to sit up higher, to see everything, and really be a part of it all, catching rays and enjoying the total experience.

JD, Kyle, and I traveled to REI and looked at several boats, discussing their design. We spotted an Advanced Elements inflatable kayak and pumped it up in the bike room. We determined how we could position Kyle's hips so he could sit in the kayak, and it worked to perfection. We bought the boat on the spot and were now adequately outfitted to do triathlons.

Since Kyle had never been on the open water, JD suggested that we take him out on the lake to prepare him for all the things that could go right and wrong during the race. Ben Franklin once said, "Those who fail to plan, plan to fail," and we were all about planning, safety, and preparation. John David had taken Kyle on kayak trips, but Kyle had always been nestled down deep in the boat. We wanted to position him at a higher angle so that he could witness what was going on around him, but this exposed him a bit more, making tipping more possible.

We went out to a lake near Kennesaw State, and I got in the water with Kyle in the kayak. John David said, "We need to flip the boat. We need to see what happens with Kyle if he falls out. If the kayak flips and Kyle is still in it, we are all in trouble." We flipped the boat, and sure enough, Kyle went facedown into the water. We got to him quickly, and he was simultaneously coughing and laughing. We realized that if anything happened, we would only have twenty to thirty seconds to get to him, perhaps less. I was nervous, and I know my mom was really freaked out about it, but Kyle wanted to be a triathlete. We felt comfortable that we had the right boat and that we were prepared for the race. We felt that all the extra training and preparedness was going to get us across the finish line.

As the plan came together, we needed help in many ways. We eventually found several additional sponsors to help make our dream a reality.

As race day neared, the coordination that would be needed seemed out of control. How do we get an eighty-five-pound bike to Florida? How do we get the boat and jogger down with just the family van? Eventually, we received a donation of a trailer, complete with all the sponsor logos, for the seven-and-a-half-hour trek to St. Petersburg. Without this overwhelming support, we would have been dead in the water.

The trio of Pease brothers had set their sights on the St Anthony's Triathlon in St. Petersburg, Florida for several reasons. The proximity of St Anthony's made it the correct choice for our first triathlon. It was a popular race, with a population of about 4,000-plus runners competing on a relatively flat course. We wanted to make sure that completing the race itself, not the course or conditions, was the biggest challenge before we took off the training wheels and increased the obstacles. We don't always have the luxury to control those conditions, however; we ended up battling the heat and the current after all.

We always knew we were going to progress from shorter triathlon distances to our long-term goal of doing an IRONMAN. This was how our dream began, and we weren't going to let go of it until we completed an IRONMAN distance triathlon. I had always been meticulous in my planning, and I didn't want to jump right into an IRONMAN. As with any quest, you set your sights on the final destination, but need to learn from the experience along the way. Successes and failures are necessary to build your toolbox. Without the necessary tools, it is unlikely you will be able to navigate the challenges an IRONMAN is likely to present.

We had put so much energy into our preparation. I had spent weeks in the water with a five-gallon bucket tied to my waist, swimming with it to mimic pulling weight. We did that for one hour, once a week. After the St Anthony's triathlon, we stopped using the bucket as a training tool, as we found that it was much heavier than the boat and Kyle in tandem. It certainly got me prepared to pull Kyle, but it turned out to be overpreparation and unnecessary.

To prepare for the bike side, I did a lot of biking. I would go up into the mountains of Georgia and ride for miles upon miles. I used the same course for my run training and logged more miles than I care to count. We were initially only training for the Charles Harris 10K, yet I was running eight to twelve miles leading up to it. We also had the Publix Half Marathon on our schedule, so all of this was part of our preparation for that and St Anthony's as well.

Kyle and I trained together on several two-hour runs on the five-mile track at Columns Drive. We could do loops there, and Evan would come over to do some of the run with us. I sensed that the triathlon was going to take a physical toll on Kyle, and I wanted him to be part of the training. It would've been very easy for me to say, "I'm doing all the physical training and Kyle will just show up on race day and sit in his chair," but that was never the point of this. We were looking to do something together, to be athletes together. That was the biggest part of this entire journey. We've since learned that competing is far more than just having Kyle along for the ride. Like any athlete, his pulse quickens, his lungs fill with oxygen, he perspires, and he needs to prepare for and recover from an event. As mentally healthy as it is for a disabled athlete to compete, it is also an extremely positive physical experience. It is so much more than sitting in a chair and watching the scenery pass by.

This was not much different than when the three of us would play baseball in our back yard. It would have been easy for us to stick Kyle behind the catcher and tell him he was the umpire, but we'd committed to making him part of the experience. We'd gone to Sports Authority and gotten him a bunch of umpire gear, but whenever we could, with the help of Dad, we pushed him around the bases, and helped him belt homeruns over that short right-field fence. Doing that was a way for Kyle to get into it, to really be a part of the action. By doing the 10K, the Publix Half Marathon, and training for St Anthony's, he was slowly becoming engaged in this process, too. If you want to be a triathlete, you need to train to be a triathlete.

CHAPTER 10

St Anthony's Triathlon: The Dawn of a New Athlete

Brent, Kyle, and Evan

"When I'm out there with Kyle, sometimes I forget that there's this extra weight. Kyle borrows my legs and I borrow his spirit and you know, that really helps us get through it."

- Brent Pease

Kyle

With about a week to go before we traveled to Florida, I confided in Brent that I was extremely excited and even a little nervous, as any athlete would be prior to a major event. I felt nervous because I had never done anything like this before but assured him that I was 100% confident in the equipment, and most of all, in his strength and ability. With a vote of confidence like that, Brent said he knew we would successfully complete the course.

Not much had changed for Brent in terms of the actual working out, but he'd quickly added more volume and done more functional strength training to help prepare for our first race together. Physically, he was ready. Mentally, I had to get myself to the same place.

Heading down to the race was a great experience for me. I talked with Brent about our nutrition plan, provided to us by Coach Matthew Rose. I also relaxed with Sam while we took our time getting to St. Petersburg.

As we went over our walk-through on Saturday, I could tell the extra strength training Brent had completed was paying off for him. He looked and felt ready for Sunday, and this helped put my mind at ease. After dinner with our friends from Tri-Kids and a few laughs amongst friends, I was off to bed to get ready for Sunday.

Our first St Anthony's was one of those iconic races, because people would witness us doing the entire triathlon. It wasn't our first race, as we had already done Charles Harris and then Publix, but it was our first triathlon. It was in the ocean, and it was intimidating. All our family was there, and the support really meant a lot.

My day started at 4:40 on Sunday morning, when Sam started getting me dressed for the big day. I woke up and shared with Sam and my aides, Amy and Kelsey, that I was not mentally ready and that I did not want to go through with it. These were just the butterflies talking. This was a long-time dream, and sometimes when you are standing on the edge of the shore and you know the water is going to be cold, it's difficult to uncurl your toes from the sand and jump in. They kept pushing me, telling me it was time to go and that I had to go through with my dream.

We grabbed a quick breakfast and I spent some alone time with my iPod, listening to one of my favorite Widespread Panic songs, "Walkin," as it reminds me of our theme, "Walking with KPeasey."

The wind that morning was intense, coming in off the water at about twenty miles per hour. I was a little nervous at that point, and it didn't help when the swim portion of the race was moved to a different location at the last minute to protect not only me, but all athletes, against the ferocious surf. I had butterflies in my stomach. I was so nervous that the waves would knock me over, I kept telling Brent and Evan that I was feeling unsure if this was the right time and place for me to begin my athletic endeavor. My brothers helped calm me down, encouraged me to take a few deep breaths, and we headed to the start.

Perhaps to bring levity to every stressful situation, I got a message quite loud and clear from high above. As we were getting situated with the boat, a bird flew overhead and pooped on me. It splattered everywhere and helped to ease a bit of the nervous anxiety I was experiencing. Once I was loaded in the boat, the waves started crashing against the shore, making me nervous again, but I was out of time. The race was going on with or without me, and I just wasn't missing out on this. This was far bigger a stage than Charles Harris or even the Publix Half Marathon. The race was so big; everyone was lined up on the sea wall, and with us going first, they would see us take off together. I was racing, no matter what came my way, and it was time to face the day.

The gun went off, marking the start of my dream, and we were off. It felt like I was sitting five feet above the water at times, as I watched Brent push through the swim. I held my breath and began saying prayers because I didn't want the kayak to tip over. We were about 300 feet into the water before I started to relax, but I ultimately did, and really began to enjoy the experience. I couldn't really see much, since I had so much water in my eyes from all the splashing swimmers around us, but it was still like a dream come true. I tried to focus on the experience, but I went into a bit of a daydream at the thought of what I was experiencing. When I'd mentioned IRONMAN in Louisville in between bites of Brent's long-awaited burger, I'd known that this was what I wanted to do, but accomplishing it was more than I could have ever imagined. If I had the ability to pinch myself, I certainly would have, to assure myself this was real, and not a figment of my imagination.

The swim distance was shortened to about 600 yards and was as much an emotional journey as a physical one. I kept thinking, *please don't tip over, please carry me home, Brent.* I prayed. I cheered. I focused intently on the tasks at hand. Water in my eyes again, Evan cheering and grabbing the boat from Brent. Here we go. The swim seemed like it flew by, but I knew our day was just beginning.

As we came in, we heard the crowd encouraging us and the other swimmers. Brent did an amazing job on the swim and kept the energy going into the other two events, a 24.2 mile bike ride, and a 10K run.

Evan was the first person we saw as we came in out of the water. He lifted me out of the kayak, got me into the wheelchair, and then pushed me up to the bike. The crowd was going crazy, and it really gave me a lot of energy. As we moved through the chains towards the bike, I looked back at Evan one more time, wishing he'd come along for our ride, too. It was so great to experience my first triathlon with both of my heroes, my brothers, and I appreciated every second of those early races.

As the cheers subsided, it was time for Brent and me to do the work. We had a long bike ride to complete in the Florida wind and heat. Thankfully, we had a motorcycle escort to go with us.

We transitioned to the bike as quickly as possible and Brent and I headed out. There were many other riders telling us what a great job we were doing and that we inspired them. To me, I was just Kyle, but hearing that I was an inspiration to others really felt incredible. Brent helped me to stay extremely hydrated on the bike to make sure I was prepared for the rest of the day. I was in front of Brent, who would take a drink himself and then reach over my head and squirt water into my mouth during the ride. This was the first bike Freedom Concepts put together for us. It was quite heavy and didn't have many gears, but it got the job done. We had a good time along the way and talked to each other throughout the course. Many people think that Brent is at a disadvantage, pulling the weight of his brother and an oversized bike, but we decided long ago that having the ability to talk with each other during the event is an advantage that others don't enjoy. Brent and Curtis were also focused on making me the cyclist. Putting me up front allows me to feel the wind in my face and to feel the race rolling out in front of me. Besides, if I had to gaze at Brent's backside all day, I might catch some of his wind. I had way more fun on the front, and it was hard work up there, too.

My position on the bike was amazing, and it was one of the few times racing that I was the most comfortable there. As the bike changed, so too did the work I had to do, but let's come back to that later. I love being in front of the bike, helping Brent get 400 pounds moving through the day, working together, and just being out there with all the other athletes. I also learned that many athletes pee themselves during races rather than taking the time to stop. When in Rome, you do what the Romans do, so I figured, why not do the same? I relieved myself at mile twenty, causing Brent and I to laugh at the thought that I had been pooped on and peed on, all within the first twenty-one miles of the event.

As we began our final mile of the ride, Brent reminded me to stay calm and wait to release all my adrenaline during the run portion. He exhibited such strength out on the bike. There were a couple hills that slowed us down, but overall, we kept up a great pace and finished in a little over two hours. There was a crowd of people waiting to help us get out of the bike and ready for the run. Evan was warming up his legs so that all three of the Pease brothers could run the 10K together.

St Anthony's was a special event. It was quite surreal to have both of my brothers cross the finish with me, and it brought me instantly back to the games we played together at our home, in our driveway, in our back yard, and on the field as young kids. This was different, though, as I wasn't competing in a sport with different rules to accommodate me. I was competing against real athletes, playing by the very same rules.

Toward the end of the race, I could taste the finish. I was so pumped up that I arched my back, pointed my face skyward, and screamed with excitement. I cannot put into words how it felt to cross the finish line and call myself a triathlete alongside my two amazing brothers.

To see their three sons cross the finish line together meant so much to my parents, who beamed with happiness accompanied by a steady flow of tears. Over the years, my mom and dad never took no for an answer, teaching my brothers and me the same very valuable lesson. Crossing the finish line with Evan and Brent was a perfect, defining moment.

Evan

I didn't arrive in St. Petersburg until late on Friday evening, super tired from my week. My exhaustion hindered some of my excitement until I got to dinner and felt the breeze from the ocean. I really felt the rush of enthusiasm that you can only get from a race like this. Saturday was a whirlwind of a day for us as we prepped for the race. I walked with Brent around eight to check out the water and to keep an eye on him during a warm-up swim. The surf was incredible, and I wasn't sure that Kyle would be safe riding around in waves that were white capped and cresting consistently. Brent disappeared about one-hundred yards from the beach because the surf was so high.

Following the practice swim, we got on our bike. I had a bad feeling as we struggled to get the bike tuned up for the race. By ten-thirty, the heat was beating down on us, and I realized we would be running in the same type of heat the next day. We finally took some practice laps with the bike, and then with the jogger, to shore up our preparation.

Saturday afternoon was my favorite time of the weekend, as unusual as that sounds. We sat down with reporter Matt Pearl for the final segment of our three-part interview for Atlanta television station 11Alive, which included plenty of cutting up and total relaxation, before heading to the hotel and catching a great night's sleep.

Race day was a bit anxious for me. I was not joining the boys until the run, but I really wanted them to do well. As they came back in from the bike, it was nearing ninety degrees, and I had been waiting to start running for more than two hours. One of my favorite parts of the run was when some of our friends from Dynamo Multisport ran alongside us, rooting us on. Our coach, Matthew Rose, and our training partner, Erik Johnson, ran twice the length of the course just to catch us at every turn. The extra effort on their part really helped push us through that final stretch.

Crossing the finish line is difficult to describe. We were sprinting and cheering to the finish before we were swarmed by our friends and family. It was just the way I wanted it to end. Kyle was so excited, it made any aches go away. After a few beers at lunch, we were ready for the next race.

BRENT

We arrived on Friday and went down to register for the race. People kept asking Kyle if he was part of the Pease family. It was exciting that people were expecting us, and the folks from St Anthony's Triathlon were incredibly accommodating and helpful. We had to register Kyle for a day pass to the USAT (governing body for triathlons). Something told me we wouldn't be needing day passes for very long, but rather the annual pass instead. After we registered, we waited for the rest of the family to show up and prepared for our race.

On Saturday morning, we prepared the bike and jogger. I was glad we did the equipment check, though, as it gave us all a level of comfort for Sunday's race. As we readied ourselves for bed, I was reminded of something one of our friends told us: "No matter how much you plan the race, it goes down the way it is supposed to go down." That statement could not have been more accurate.

As we awoke on race day, Evan and I prepared all our nutrition and fluids and headed toward transition. As soon as we got there, though, we were informed the swim start had been moved due to the high winds.

I got a bout of nervous energy almost instantly, and made some quick calls to alert Kyle and ask the rest of our family to bring him all the way to transition for a revised swim start. Once Kyle arrived, he looked a little nervous, and all I kept thinking was that we had to remain calm and let the day play out the way it was supposed to play out. As we readied the boat, a nice calm started to set in. I knew in an instant it would be just me and my brothers on the road, and that was it. As the horn sounded,

I took off on the swim, and settled in for the day.

Being out there with Kyle was amazing. I couldn't believe how light the boat felt. I got excited, took a few glances back at Kyle, and before I knew it, the swim was over. As soon as I got out of the water, Evan was with us, helping get Kyle squared away for the jog back to transition.

As we headed out for the bike course, the crowd was amazing—not only our friends and family, but also all the other spectators. They rooted us on, and their energy was something else. As Kyle and I headed out on the bike, I encouraged him to just relax and save it for the final stretch of the run. It was going to be a long day, and we were just getting going.

The bike was amazing. Freedom Concepts had Kyle comfortable on a bike that was ready for a race. What might have been the best part of the bike portion was being able to enjoy the ride with Kyle. We had never done anything like that before. When we were kids, we used to have to put Kyle inside a buggy behind the bike, and never got to enjoy the rides with him. Today was different, though, as we flew across the road. Before we knew it, Evan was grabbing the bike from us and helping push us back to the run.

The run was hot, but Kyle was pretty settled in for a race to the finish. Evan and I kept talking with Kyle to make sure to make sure he had enough nutrition and fluids on the run. This would always be critical for Kyle. IRONMAN and all these events are long and hard on his body, just like they are on all the other athletes. He must pay attention, too, and ensure we all do our part. As the miles started ticking away, we got closer to our goal of completing our first triathlon as brothers.

I'm not sure how to describe the finish line, but it was a feeling unlike any other. Our feet seemed to get lighter, and we found that extra kick to blaze across the line. Everyone had worked so hard just to get to the starting line, and from that moment to the very end, we'd been working together. As we all lay exhausted near the finish, before the dust had even settled, Kyle asked, "What's next?" In the same way that a first race impacts everyone who races, this finish left Kyle hungry for more.

Finishing the race together is a memory that will stay with me forever.

The three of us crossed the line together, exactly three hours and thirty-four minutes after the start of our wave. When we hit the finish, the announcer called out Kyle's name. It was unbelievable. Kyle let loose a scream like you'd never heard before.

CHAPTER 11

The Birth of the Foundation

Brent

"It's all about being out there with my brother, support-
ing each other, and helping other people with disabil-
ities to show them that anything is possible."

- Kyle Pease

U pon finishing St Anthony's, Kyle exclaimed that he wanted others
to experience this feeling, too. He didn't feel disabled. He felt like a
triathlete. There was no asterisk next to his name, no label, just a medal
draped around his neck and the excitement that all athletes feel after
a big accomplishment. We thought he wanted more people to run with
him. My initial reaction was that he was alluding to our need for more
Pease brothers to help us complete the race. At Mom and Dad's ages, it
was quite clear that was not going to happen, so I humorously thought
maybe Kyle was suffering from dehydration. I soon realized that he was
speaking about expanding the opportunity to others and starting a

foundation. Kyle knew at that moment that he wanted to create a foundation to provide opportunities for others to experience the feeling of inclusion that he had just experienced.

Following our physical recovery from St Anthony's, the discussions became less about what race we would do next and more about how to give other kids the opportunity to do what we do. I wasn't so sure that this would ever come to fruition, seeing it as more of a whim that Kyle would soon grow tired of. Kyle really wanted to do it, though, and I was trying hard not to be the big brother. I promised myself that I would not tell him what we should and shouldn't do. I just let him work through it, put his preliminary plans together, and sure enough, he did.

Prior to doing some research, we believed that we were the only people competing as duo athletes. Following the race, we delved a bit deeper, and learned that this was not the case. There was enough news coverage and stories throughout the Internet about similar groups that people started to reach out to tell us about groups in several different areas around the country, groups like Team Hoyt in Virginia, myTeam Triumph, Athletes Serving Athletes, and Ainsley's Angels. Learning that there might already be a blueprint for us to follow and other groups in existence providing the same experiences to disabled people excited us. We wouldn't need to reinvent the wheelchair, so to speak, but could follow the trail of those who blazed it before us. We made the decision to travel to Virginia Beach to compete in a half marathon with Team Hoyt Virginia Beach. Kyle and I, along with about fifteen other duo teams, enjoyed the 13.1-mile experience through scenic Virginia Beach. This was an eye-opening experience, as it allowed us to realize the full potential of all this. There was a bigger mission to be accomplished than just a group of brothers out playing in their backyard. The opportunity was there to invite others over to play with us as well.

At the time, I was still working in property management, and wasn't ready to get out of the real estate field just yet. I was struggling at the job, not just financially, but personally and professionally. As much as I knew I didn't want to remain in the industry long-term, it was a flexible job that allowed me to get in my training and now would afford me the opportunity to sneak in some minor foundation work at the same time.

I had an attorney friend, Drew Marler, with whom I occasionally ran, who helped us with all the paperwork necessary to establish an official nonprofit. We had zero idea how to even begin such an undertaking, so his guidance was invaluable. We met at his law firm, and Kyle invited all his buddies, hand-selected to make up our first official board of directors. We didn't realize it initially, but we were just a bunch of guys in our early-twenties with no money and no real professional networking experience joined together by a common desire. Most of us had five years or less of exposure to the business world. What we did have was heart, energy, and a love of one common denominator—Kyle Pease. It might not have been the smartest idea to think we could launch a real foundation, but somehow, some way, we pooled our hearts, our enthusiasm, and our love of KPeasey, and got things off the ground. All the people who were there at the beginning of KPF helped us get where we are today. Without their guidance, their enthusiasm, and their support, we wouldn't have accomplished nearly what we have.

At that first meeting, I had to sit on my hands and bite my lip so I didn't take over for Kyle or step on his dream. This was his vision, and he told us what he wanted to do to make it a reality. He wanted people to join us, and we all felt inspired by his mission. We listened intently and offered a few suggestions throughout the evening. No one had any objections to naming it The Kyle Pease Foundation or any argument about his mission statement. And that was it. The Kyle Pease Foundation was launched that very evening in a lawyer's office by a bunch of guys wearing jeans and t-shirts. We were off to the races and ready to get all the paperwork completed to make it all official.

In June, after all the paperwork was completed and filed, we received our 501(c)(3) approval from the IRS and needed to sit down and figure out exactly what we had just done. We set up a meeting with Michael Lenhart, who had experience with a nonprofit called Getting2Tri. Mike had helped double-amputee and Georgia native Scott Rigsby get to Kona to compete in the IRONMAN World Championship in 2007, and was extremely knowledgeable in the nonprofit world. We met up with him at Taco Mac for the first time. He greeted us by saying, "Well, congratulations. You guys now own a business." We both looked at each other, shrugged our shoulders and said, "Oh crap. We do?"

Mike believed we were on the right path, and fortunately he was willing to help us dot the i's, cross the t's, and get to the next level of readiness. By November, we were ready to officially launch the foundation and start fundraising. For what? We weren't quite sure, but we knew that in order to achieve our goals, we needed money. Kyle and I competed in a few more races over the coming months and spent much of our time trying to do outreach. We contacted the Atlanta Track Club in hopes of gaining admittance into the historic Peachtree Road Race and did whatever we could to put ourselves in front of a wide audience. We figured that with exposure, we were sure to attract both athletes and donations. Though we were correct, it wasn't quite as easy as that.

We thought, if you build it, they will come, but it wasn't always that easy. We needed to get the message out about our mission and find some people as adventurous as Kyle looking for more inclusive opportunities. We had only enough equipment to support the races that Kyle and I were doing, not to equip other future athletes. The goal of the foundation is to support and enrich the lives of other people with disabilities through racing. Without at least a small fleet of race chairs, it was going to be difficult to include others.

In 2009, Kyle wanted to bring awareness to cerebral palsy, so he joined forces with another local CP foundation called Reaching for the Stars to host a bowling fundraiser. It was relatively easy to put on and accessible for those with disabilities, allowing everyone to have the opportunity to participate. Kyle had taken a sports marketing and management class while he was at Kennesaw State, and one of his assignments was to put on an event as a project, so this was familiar for him. He did such a good job. We should have known he would be successful with his foundation.

Following the launch of the foundation, we put on our own bowling fundraiser to raise funds for KPF. This was a solo event with proceeds going to KPF. The event was rather simple, but with Kyle's experience from 2009 and our new foundation, we were able to raise enough money to provide us with a bit of working capital. We still hold the annual event to this day, and it is our primary fundraiser during the year. I'm pleased to say that we have partnered with Kyle's old school, Kennesaw State, which offers their sports management department and one of its classes to help put on and provide the volunteer support at our annual bowling fundraiser. Without them, the event would not be nearly as well run or successful. This event has its roots in Kyle's education and is part of what funds the sixteen events we now participate in each year with KPF.

Our initial marketing technique at the start of KPF was to just go to races. So, in 2012, we set out to do one race a month. At a 10K in February, a mom came up to us and said, "Oh, my God, this is what I've been looking for. My son is in a wheelchair." She asked how they could get involved. I got excited and told her that our foundation could help her and her son. We invited her to our next board meeting.

On a cold night in February, Amy Vinson came all the way down from Alpharetta to this little law firm where we were holding our board meetings. She sat down with her son, Jake, in her lap, and told us their story. We were all on the verge of tears and wanted to do anything we could to help. The faith her family put in us allowed us to serve our first athlete, Jake Vinson. He'd been injured in a pond a few years before we met him and was very limited in communication. When they ran with us, Jake's mom said she had never seen so much life in his eyes. I think Kyle's relationship with the family was also something very special. Kyle knew there was something that he could give to them, and that meant a lot.

Finding Jake was a giant relief. We had been working for nine months as a foundation, and, in our minds, we had nothing to show for it. We wanted to share what we experienced at St Anthony's and Publix, and the Vinsons gave us that opportunity. We wanted to show them how special these races are, and The Kyle Pease Foundation played a role in giving them that experience.

We signed the Vinsons up for the Publix 5K, and on that Saturday in 2012, Kyle and I went down to Centennial Park with them to cheer them on. We waited with them at the start, and right before the race began, we decided to run with them. We were doing a half marathon the next day, so initially had no intention of doing the 5K, but that didn't matter. We were the last ones to finish. We ended up running; that competitive spirit that we share kicked in, and we took off a little on the last mile.

Amy Vinson had this amazing experience with her son and really wanted to do it again. She also wanted to get all her friends involved. They'd been looking for a way to help her cope and to be involved with her son, and this was the way that would come to mean so much to her. Here she was, a mom with a son who'd had a traumatic brain injury at eighteen months, going from being an able-bodied kid to a child with a disability in the blink of an eye.

The experience was magical for all of us. Kyle and I were providing an experience for a family in need, and Amy and Jake were helping to establish us as a foundation. We were no longer just two brothers racing together. We were responsible for other athletes as well.

Jake became our very first athlete in March 2012, and we were finally putting our money to work. We were buying extra equipment and doing races. After Jake joined us, the athletes started coming to us in waves. First, we met Greg Smith and his daughter, Marin. We had little idea how large a role Greg would play—for both of us as a friend, but also for all KPF and the mission of inclusion. They joined us for a 5K in June of 2012, and along with Jake, we had our largest race to date. Little precocious Marin told her daddy to go faster as she squealed with delight. Then we were joined by Justin Knight, aka JDude, and before we knew it, we had five athletes. Then, in a flash, we had twelve. It happened rather quickly after Jake.

I guess that once you build it, they really do come. Someone just forgot to tell us about all the hard work that comes first, but we needed to go through it to truly learn those lessons. Just like becoming an IRONMAN, it does not happen overnight.

That next month, Kyle and I competed together in our first Half IRONMAN in New Orleans. We were the last ones to finish after more than seven-and-a-half hours of racing. We had made some improvements to the bike, but it was still an eight gear, 400-pound behemoth of steel and human. It was so cold and windy that, at times, we could barely go six miles per hour on the flat roads of New Orleans. Kyle was so tough that day as the steel dug into his legs and cut his skin. As the wind whipped in his face, he calmly implored me to press forward. This was the team. This was what it took to continue. Coming in on the bike, most of the people were already finished with their day. As we started onto the run course, it began to get really hot. We took off Kyle's jacket, but forgot about sunscreen. He didn't ask to stop. He wanted to pass all those folks that had passed us on the bike. He begged me to keep going, told me not to give up.

As we neared the finish, I noticed it was pretty empty, but I ran harder as Kyle let out some weak cheers. We were both near exhaustion, and as we crossed the line, the announcer bellowed out, "Brothers from Atlanta, Kyle and Brent Pease!" The only cheers were from our family and Kyle's aides. I hugged Kyle as the tears started to flow. The emotional purge of pressing on from the edge of exhaustion is part of what brings me here. It's part of what I hope to share with Kyle. When we looked down, we took stock of the damage. We were both sunburned, but Kyle's skin was bubbling. He was beaming, however, with his shiny new medal hanging around his charbroiled neck. We had competed with everyone, on the same course, and had our first "endurance race" under our belt. It provided Kyle and me with another tool for our ever-growing toolbox.

We held true to our plan, doing one race every month for the balance of the year. We did three triathlons and several running races, including the Thanksgiving Day half marathon. The Atlanta Track Club was still trying to determine how best to accommodate teams like us. So, in lieu of Peachtree that year, we ran in the annual Thanksgiving Classic to give the Atlanta Track Club a taste of how it would all come together. We were joined by good buddy Kevin Enners, and Greg Smith came out to run with us as well. The half marathon was a good way to get in a long run before going home to crush some turkey. It was a better way to teach the Atlanta running community about inclusion and hopefully open more doors for us and the athletes of KPeasey.

Accomplishing this goal was a big deal for us. This was the first year we did the Holcomb Bridge Hustle, where we met Justin Knight, another one of the athletes who is still a huge part of our foundation. We started the Jake Vinson Family Grant to honor Jake after he passed away, to show that he is still, and will always be, a part of the foundation. We met so many wonderful people in those early years who had, and continue to have, a profound impact on the foundation. Each and every athlete, as well as their families, becomes part of our family and our personal stories. It is so different from running a business where you accumulate customers or clients. With every new athlete, we create a story and make a new group of friends that will forever become part of the lore of The Kyle Pease Foundation, and leave an everlasting imprint on our hearts.

Last year's speaker at the Marine Corps Marathon spoke about this very topic and noted that The Kyle Pease Foundation feels like a family. It's more than just running 5Ks and 10Ks with a group of strangers. Amy and Scott Vinson made us more than that. By allowing us to help her, she helped us become what we are and what we were intended to be. We were now truly helping people. It was more than just two brothers racing, more than just us chasing finish lines. It was now the collective we, and we always knew we could do so much more together. The Vinsons played such a big role in that and continue to do so today. The mission began after our first triathlon and as big as our goals may have been, they were rivaled closely by that of those we hoped to be able to serve.

Kyle and I were still young guys at that point, trying to figure out what the heck we were trying to accomplish. We had a dream and a vision but were not sure how to get there. Jake's mom, Amy, and Justin's mom, Teresa, realized we were just two brothers with a close bond, but they let us into their lives and placed enough trust in our vision to allow us to help them. That is what made us all family. Even as we have grown, we still maintain that bond, with each other and with the families of the foundation, and that has been the most incredible part of this experience.

Initially, we had established The Kyle Pease Foundation Family Grant as a way to support our athletes outside of the racing arena. After Jake passed away, Kyle and I both felt that we wanted to rename the grant after him. The first recipient was Jessica Minton, followed by Justin Knight, Sherry Adams, Noah Williams, Cougar Clifford and finally, Lizzie Kirksey. This list will continue to grow and honor the memory of our first athlete and his wonderful family.

The Vinsons were very touched. It was not anything they ever would have asked us to do, not anything they needed—they are not people who seek to be noticed. It was just something nice that we could do to show them how much Jake meant to us, and that he and his family would always be a part of the foundation. The Vinsons are still very much a part of the foundation. Amy is a member of our selection committee for the Jake Vinson Grant, and is also involved with a group that works closely with families of people with traumatic brain injuries. She brings families from this network to experience KPF and solicits her friends to help push them.

Upon officially establishing the foundation, race directors weren't always sure how to work with us. Many race directors would not allow strollers. While they were just trying to be safe for parents wanting to push kids, they were not making reasonable accommodations for those who could not self-propel. Kyle is one of the most competitive athletes I know and why should he just have to sit and watch? Our work expanded to advocate for those race opportunities and create chances that weren't there before. We never forgot the instance when a race director told us begrudgingly that we could race together, but that we had to finish in under sixty minutes. We finished that day in forty-seven minutes, and the last time we ran there, it was just over thirty-seven minutes. It was never easy. The New York Marathon was a four-year process, IRONMAN nearly six years. The obstacles for inclusion are many and it will be a continuing process of education. It's hard being constantly told you do not belong. We have all been in situations like that, but this started as early as kindergarten for Kyle, when he was told he didn't belong in a regular classroom. We certainly hope, as we show up to an event with over sixty wheelchairs or as directors see amazing athletic feats by those who do not seem "capable," that the struggles will be minimized. It is our aim not to just provide an experience to and beyond the finish line, but a chance to show others what a truly inclusive start line looks like. While much work has been done, there is still more work needed to continue to open doors for other athletes. Some directors are easier to work with than others, and we continue to seek out relationships that will allow those races and directors to flourish, while allowing our families the best opportunities for success.

Early races like Publix, the Holcomb Bridge Hustle, St Anthony's, and the Charles Harris welcomed us right away. Those first few races are special to us for the access they gave and for their generosity. They helped us as we were learning. We stay true to them because they are special, not only to the organization, but also to Kyle and me personally.

At our first Publix race, we were the only team running. Now there are about sixty teams, and single athletes with disabilities competing using handcycles. The Summerfest race is a local 5K that had no other athletes with disabilities the first year we competed. The next year, there were four athletes in wheelchairs there, not associated with the foundation. The race director had the wherewithal to establish a wheelchair category based on what he had witnessed the year prior. We made a positive impact on that race.

KYLE

This is the primary reason I ultimately started The Kyle Pease Foundation. I wanted to help people to find their voice. I believe we all have a voice, whether we can physically speak or not, and it's up to us to advocate for ourselves and for each other. We all play a part in the life of a person who needs more assistance than we do. We need to take a step back on occasion and realize how grateful we should be when we are able to be that person for somebody else.

Near the end of 2014, Greg encouraged Brent to become the full-time executive director of KPF. Brent had been managing a lot of the duties of an executive director for KPF, along with back-office tasks, so it was a natural fit and I was really pumped for him. It wasn't always an easy road for him, though. In 2016, when his daughter Caroline was just six months old, Brent and Erica moved into her parents' basement to save some money. So much commitment to KPeasey, and so much dedication from his wife and family. They really wanted this to work, we all did, but it takes a real sacrifice to relocate into your in-law's basement with a newborn to try to make it happen. We all did whatever we could to keep this train rolling. That first board of directors, leaders like Greg, and now even JDude and Kevin, manage components of KPF from their wheelchairs. Brent gets some credit though. I am not sure if Kona would happen if he was still trying to make ends meet with our "startup." I hope to join him as an employee of KPF one day soon as well. I'm just not sure if I will be living in a basement to make that work. For now, I am proud to say that our family, KPeasey, is able to make a huge impact because so many sacrificed so much in those early years.

When I launched The Kyle Pease Foundation, I wanted others to have their own defining moment and to experience a starting line and a finish line, both on the race course and in life. Especially for a person with a disability, every day is a marathon. In many ways, it's a more difficult race than 26.2 miles. There is no quitting at the halfway point, no matter how much you hurt, despite the pain and the challenge. There is no better feeling of accomplishment than breaking the metaphorical tape and crossing the finish line. The marathon each of us experiences is only different in that there is usually no one at the finish line each day to cheer us on. It's a race we run daily simply by choosing to compete.

CHAPTER 12

THE LANDS OF PEACH TREES
AND CHEESE HEADS

BRENT

"Inspiration at its best. The IRONMAN was the epitome of physical and mental dedication being manifested in one day of truly hard work between two outstanding brothers."

- SAM HARRISON

I n many ways, Kona reminds me of my whole life, the challenges I've faced on a day-to-day basis. I sit in a wheelchair for sixteen to eighteen hours a day, but when I do the IRONMAN, I'm being moved around a lot and experiencing things I am not normally accustomed to. It wears me out. Even though Brent is doing the physical work, it takes a big toll on me as well.

All week, we were treated like rock stars. From foundation events to press panels and even a chance to sit with Bob Babbitt, a legend in the IRONMAN Hall of Fame. Everywhere we went felt like the Super Bowl. So much to see and so much to do. We always left plenty of time for rest, hydration, and nutrition, *however. We were here to finish the drill. To hoist our own Lombardi trophy. This was similar to the Super Bowl as well in that the team that can put the distractions aside and focus on the game at hand has the best opportunity to succeed.*

We spent some additional time during the week practicing with the bike out on the Queen K Highway. Since the bike was a new version, we needed to learn as much as we could about how it performed and how to keep me comfortable for the eight to nine-hour duration of the ride. We were loose and enjoyed some great conversation, but it also gave us an idea of what we were up against. We got to experience the heat and the hills and the intense cross winds that we'd be experiencing on race day. Because the temperatures were so hot, we could see the heat radiating from the pavement, which was something I'd never really witnessed before. There were so many new experiences that accompanied the trip that, even though we had competed in several IRONMAN events before this, it really felt like our first time competing.

We initially looked into running the Peachtree in 2011 and then asked again in 2012. Both times, we were denied entry. Though there were dozens of self-propelled wheelchairs and handcycle competitors, the race organizers were hesitant to open the doors to a team like Kyle and me.

I think they finally realized that we weren't going away. To be fair to the Atlanta Track Club, it was not because they didn't want us to participate, they just didn't know how to make the logistics of it work. Just like many other races, including Boston and New York, there are rules that require participants to cross the finish line under their own power. The original intent was to keep from having thousands of parents pushing strollers through a course with 60,000 other runners. But what happens when a person like Kyle with physical disabilities wants to compete? They had to revisit those rules and look at them from a different perspective.

Finally, in 2013, they accepted us into the Peachtree as a pilot, to see how it would all work. We met with Tracy, the executive director at Atlanta Track Club (ATC) and Becky at Shepherd Spinal Center. Tracy worked in conjunction with the Shepherd Center to run the wheelchair division of the Peachtree Road Race, and adding us to the wheelchair division was like controlled involvement at first. They already had sixty wheelchairs in the race, along with 60,000 people running. They had to be able to responsibly control that kind of crowd. They had to figure out how they would handle it when fifty more teams like us wanted to participate.

They came up with some rules for the two of us for this pilot run. Kyle had to wear a helmet, and we had to do everything that all the other wheelchairs were going to do. We were more than willing to do anything that they asked of us. So, they established the rules, and we were ready to race.

It was a little overcast and drizzling a bit, but we got to run the race that we had grown up with. Our mom used to run the Peachtree with her friends, so as kids, we would walk from our house up through Piedmont Park just to see her finishing and watch the wheelchair athletes come through. We didn't really think about it at the time, but looking back, the first race we ever really wanted to do was the Peachtree, the largest 10K in the world, with 60,000 people, and the race we grew up watching. And now we could promote inclusion through that race.

The foundation was growing, everything was great, and we had people there to cheer us on. I remember crossing the finish line and a woman from Fox 5 ran over to us. No one was expecting us; since it was a pilot program, there hadn't been any special promotion about us. We crossed the finish line and everyone wanted to interview us. They wanted to know the story behind these two guys pushing and pulling each other through the course. People were caught off guard at first, but that actually gave us the first round of exposure as a team of brothers. That first Peachtree was special on so many levels. We never imagined that Kyle would be a triathlete or an IRONMAN growing up, or that he would ultimately be considered among the best athletes on the planet, but here we were, racing down Peachtree under clouds and rain with the biggest smiles you've ever seen. We have so many fond memories from that race allowing us to make new ones together. The next year, we were one of two teams to compete, and there has been continued controlled growth since. We hope one day that the Peachtree will open a wheelchair assist category, so that everyone who desiresto run will be allowed.

We continue to enjoy working with Atlanta Track Club and being a part of the Atlanta running community. In 2015, Tracy left to go to work with the LA Marathon. We'd built a relationship with her and hated to see her go—we felt like we were losing an advocate. The new race director, Rich, came in, and he was equally fantastic. He loved people being involved in the running community, so he wanted to figure out how to keep making team involvement a positive experience. In his first year, he asked us if we would mind keeping it to just the two teams from the year before, growing in the years that followed. He kept his promise and gave us steady growth. Five teams participated in the 2016 Peachtree. That was when we realized that we needed to open the race up to all.

The doors were open now. It took us four years, and though we always like things to happen faster, we also want act responsibly with all of the race directors. Kyle played a major role in getting us into the Peachtree Road race. He came to all the meetings, and they listened to his plea. When things come easily, they don't mean as much. Getting through the struggles together is the victory. With Peachtree in our rearview mirror, it was time to set our sights on our next "biggest race of our entire life," the IRONMAN Wisconsin on September 10 in Madison.

Race morning came early; as usual, my alarm was just a back-up, as I'd been up since 3:30, beginning final preparations for race day. I was more calm than normal and packed my bags to head down to the lobby. Once in the lobby, we met Kyle, Sam, Curtis, and John David. The drive over was calm, and we had every detail worked out for our day.

The swim is normally the easiest part of the day, and with all of our planning, we knew that we had everything ready. The boat had been blown up and stored the night before, so all we had to do was joke around and get ready for the race to begin. Kyle wanted to get in early so we could have some quiet time before the swim began. We loaded the boat and threw on the wetsuit. With about fifteen minutes to go until the sounding of the starter's pistol, we swam out and positioned ourselves behind the pros. (Wisconsin was an in-water start at the time, though this has since changed.)

I told Kyle that no matter what happened the rest of the day, I was proud to be out there with him and that today would be memorable. He smiled, agreed, and got the look on his face that all athletes get before the gun goes off—a look of determination. The start of an IRONMAN is always special for us. We need a village to pull this off, and at these races, there is usually quite literally a village with us. Those moments we share in private are always so special to us both.

The swim itself turned out to be trickier than expected, thanks to a strong headwind. Our kayak was as trusty as ever, and before I knew it, we were closing in on the shore. The scene after the swim is something that cannot be equaled. Upon exiting the water, you must run up a four-story helix where the crowd had been lining up for prime positioning since five in the morning. The helix is like a winding ramp as you climb levels in a parking garage, and here I am, dressed in my wetsuit, running with Kyle in my tired arms. As we climbed the helix, I watched as people just reached out to touch Kyle as he passed by. They were inspired, touched, and just plain moved by what they were witnessing. A young man who could not use his arms and legs in the water was fiercely climbing the helix with his brother. The thought of the brothers taking on 140.6 miles with 2500 other incredible people was a very moving experience for the onlookers. The sound was deafening and provided us with a burst of adrenaline as we ascended the helix and headed into transition to make our way onto the bike.

We knew the bike would be tough. IRONMAN Wisconsin is one of the more challenging bike courses there is, so before the race, Coach Matthew told us that both of us had to be prepared to dig deep into our souls, deep into our minds, and to simply find a way to get it done. The bike route contains a sixteen-mile out section, two forty-mile loops, and then sixteen miles back to transition. During the first sixteen miles, we were flying down some nice rolling hills, and with the aid of a little tailwind, were making great time. Around mile forty, it changed from rolling to steep, never-ending hills. The noise of the crowds pulled us up the hill, and we almost forgot we had to come back and do it again. When we finished the climb, we saw Matthew and Erica and told them to make sure they were there for our return lap.

I could feel the fatigue in my legs and knew it would be a battle the rest of the way. I gave Kyle some Coke, a baked potato, and a peanut butter and jelly sandwich. We had been eating every hour, but after nearly four-and-a-half hours on the bike, we wanted to load up before we got to the hills again.

I have the utmost respect for people who race in the back of the pack, because that race is all about you. You don't get the entire benefit of the crowds, because there are less people on the course, and being out there that long is hard. On lap two, it was all about Kyle and me. He pushed and pulled me around that course, screaming at me, checking the time, and helping to keep our spirits up. Matthew, Erica, JD, and Curtis were all there to help us get over the big hills. It was some of the hardest work of our day. Every fiber was burning in my legs, and all I kept thinking about was everyone who was there for us, everyone who had made this day possible, and I knew we had to finish.

We had been working to enhance the bike since New Orleans 70.3. We knew we could never finish an IRONMAN with that setup, but we were determined to keep Kyle out in front like a cyclist. Curtis Henry is a magician, and worked with Freedom Concepts on a new frame to help us build a more road-worthy bike. This finally allowed us to have a road-like setup for me and a more pronounced position for Kyle. It wasn't as comfortable for Kyle as it had been in St Anthony's, but it gave us a chance to make the challenging cutoffs in an IRONMAN. At most IRONMAN races, you have until 5:30 PM local time, or ten-and-a-half hours after you start the race, to get off the bike and make the cutoff. The bike setup in New Orleans was good, but this new one was so much better.

When we got to the top of the last hill, I was absolutely spent. I had to pedal slowly for a minute, and that's when Matthew told us, "Find something within you, Brent. Dig deep into your soul and do whatever it takes to make this bike cutoff." He told Kyle to "fight like you have never fought before to push Brent harder than he's gone," and to make sure we made the cutoff. That motivated us. However, when we turned at mile ninety, we came face-to-face with a strong headwind. *Oh crap*, I thought. *How can we do this now?* But Kyle was there, like he had been all day, to motivate and push me. He uttered a phrase that will never leave me. "I love you, Brent, but it is time to get this done. I think you can, I think you can." Just like the little engine that could, a book we loved as kids, we took it one stroke at a time. "Yes, you can. Yes, we can. Yes, I can," he told me over and over, his voice screaming into the headwind. He would not let up. Chills ran up my spine, and a lump formed in my throat. Nothing would stop us now.

After nearly nine hours on the bike, we rolled into transition. Our heads dropped, as we thought we had missed it based on the silence from the volunteers. Then a golf clap started and they told us we had made the bike cut off by just two minutes. What a relief!

While we were in transition, Kyle turned to Greg and asked if he knew the score of the Falcons game. With a wry smile, Greg shook his head no. Greg was thinking the same thing I was. *Look at this guy, middle of the biggest race of his life, and he's worried about the Falcons.* I wished the Falcons could see one of their biggest fans now. The kid that used to sweat watching games on TV was now sweating in an IRONMAN, and was still worried about the Falcons beating New Orleans. You had to laugh, and then laugh even harder, since the Saints beat us that day.

The run started off through downtown to some of the loudest cheers I have ever heard. It gave new life to my tired legs and fired us both up. I knew that together we were going to do this, and that no matter what, we were getting to the finish. We hit every aid station and loaded up on Gu, cookies, pretzels, chicken broth, and fluids. We had a big spend on that bike, and we needed all the energy we could get. Around mile eight,

I really started to struggle, and so did Kyle. I did a quick check on the math, and I knew we could walk the rest of the way and still finish, but we both knew that wasn't what we set out to do. We talked a bit, went to the bathroom, grabbed some more calories, and got moving again.

From there, adrenaline and emotions took over and I started running faster than I had at the beginning. This was actually happening. One foot in front of the other, Kyle pulling me...me pushing Kyle...together, we wheel. Together, we were going to be an IRONMAN. As we hit the midway point of the course, we went right by the finish. A volunteer looked at Kyle and smiled. Kyle looked right back and said, "I will see you later," as we ran off towards our second lap. The volunteer shouted back confidently, "You sure will."

One of the coolest moments in the race came as we entered the University of Wisconsin football stadium. The soft turf was a relief from pounding the pavement, and we fantasized that we were playing football together. It was a cool moment, with no fans and hardly anyone around. I told Kyle we were about to score, and he chuckled as we crossed the goal line and made our way towards the tunnel...one foot in front of the other.

On the last lap, Kyle and I exchanged some words. I let him know how proud I was of him. Kyle is, hands down, the toughest athlete I know, and without him, that day wouldn't have been possible. As we neared the finish, you could feel the crowd surge, and when we turned with the Capitol building at our backs, all we could hear was screaming. Kyle finally let go. I pumped my fists and allowed the accomplishment to set in. We had done something so special and were able to show everyone how powerful the mind can be. We set out to finish the race, and here we were.

We saw our mom first and gave her a big hug. Then we saw our friends and Erica. It was bedlam from that point on. I could barely hear Kyle screaming. As we hit the final stretch, I did something different. For whatever reason, I walked next to Kyle, slowly taking in that finish with him. I had always finished behind him since we started this, but now we crossed as brothers...together. As we came under the bright lights of the finish, famed announcer Mike Reilly bellowed out those famous words, "Brent

Pease and Kyle Pease, from ATLANTA...YOU ARE AN IRONMAN..."

And we were there. Medals around our neck, hugs from everyone. High-fives from Greg, photos, tears, hugs. As we sat exhausted near the finish, Matthew came by to give us both hugs. Matthew had given so much of himself to us since the beginning. He was part of what helped me turn my life in the direction I'd wanted it to go. He listened to us both, coached us both, and worked hard to make us better people, not just IRONMAN athletes. I am so proud to be your brother, Kyle Pease!

Sometimes, there are not enough words to express the gratitude we feel for those who make the biggest difference. IRONMAN Wisconsin was a total team effort. It started a long time ago, with our parents and the life they encouraged us to live, one of compassion for each other and for those around us. It continued with our friends, sponsors, and everyone who cheered us on that day. Sharing not only the race, but specifically the finish line, with Kyle is something that was truly special, and I cannot thank him and everyone enough for making such a difference.

Words Cannot Express

Greg Smith
FRIEND, SUPPORTER, AND ATHLETE

Suffering produces perseverance. Perseverance, character. Character, hope. Hope, love. Love, joy. These are all the traits embodied by Kyle and Brent that I had the honor to see play out over 140.6 miles at IRONMAN Wisconsin. To say that I am in awe of their physical and mental determination is an understatement. Watching their joy as they came down the chute, then stopped to share the final moments with Brent's wife, Erica, all of us in the Sherpa crew and 40,000 fans screaming and ringing cowbells, is a scene that will remain with me forever.

It is hard not to tear up, knowing the years of effort and preparation that went into breaking down yet another barrier, to showing the world what CAN be possible with hard work and grit. However, IRONMAN Wisconsin is so much more than witnessing the love and bonds of Brent and Kyle as they tackled this epic "suffer-fest" together as brothers. As they have said many times to anyone who will listen, their ultimate focus is on serving and helping others through The Kyle Pease Foundation. Ultimately, that's what their achievement is all about: Building the KPF team one child and adult at a time, so that those with disabilities can compete on the same stage as those who are considered able-bodied.

Kyle and Brent have demonstrated that "can do" attitude with this race, and I know their sights are set on creating additional opportunities for inclusion for other athletes as they build this team bigger and stronger. My daughter Marin and I cannot wait to don the blue shirts and race again with Kyle, Brent, and all the KPF team.

CHAPTER 13

MADISON THROUGH MY EYES

KYLE

---

*"When I see each athlete cross the finish line with a smile
on their face, that brings the greatest joy to me."*

- KYLE PEASE

I inspire myself to a certain degree when I think about being graced
with the title of IRONMAN. I am surprised that I had the strength
and the stamina to accomplish such a feat. I felt that I could do it from
a mental standpoint, but from a physical standpoint, there were many
challenges that Brent and I had to conquer. As each obstacle presented
itself, we tackled it head-on, and fought through. In many ways, being an
IRONMAN is something I am used to because of battling the everyday
challenges that accompany having cerebral palsy. Getting recognized for
such an accomplishment is beyond my wildest dreams. Being out on the
course for the fifteen hours, nine minutes, and twenty-four seconds was
both physically and emotionally grueling, but with the love and support

of my brother and my family, I leaped over each hurdle with ease.

Like Brent, I woke up way before dawn with the help of Sam, who got me dressed and grabbed my equipment for the day. I enjoyed a slice of white bread with almond butter, a banana, and a ten-ounce glass of water for my breakfast. Overall, I estimate that I drank about 300 ounces of water and peed quite a bit that day, which was very good for my body.

John David and Michael Kidd set up the kayak, while I got final instructions from Coach Matthew Rose. I needed some quiet time to gain focus because there was so much activity around us, so I asked one of my buddies to take me to a quiet area. He took me over to the water where we did a quick prayer and drank a bit more water. Greg gave me a hug and a kiss, and Michael gave me a kiss as well. I know this sounds like there was a lot of romance going on for a guy prone horizontally in a kayak, but we are a tight group and they wanted to wish me well.

Brent pulled me out into the water just behind the professionals, where I got to meet some very amazing athletes. Brent and I went over one more set of instructions, then I had to go to the bathroom on myself. This was one of nine times throughout the course of the day that I peed on myself, and though this may seem a bit graphic, it is important for readers to know what goes on behind the scenes. Being an IRONMAN comes with its downsides, and one of those downsides is the need to pee on yourself.

The cannon went off, signaling the start of the race, and we were off. People were blowing their horns and were going ballistic with enthusiasm. As we entered the back part of the swim course, I got water in my eyes. My glasses were so fogged up that I couldn't really see much. I kept screaming at Brent and listening to the surrounding noise. As the crowd noise got louder, I knew we were nearing the end of our swim. Brent said he could hear me screaming instructions the entire time in the water. Whether momentarily blind or fully sighted, I had a job to do, and like a stage actor, the show must go on. From the moment the cannon went off, I was totally engaged throughout the whole race.

We were in the water for about an hour and fifteen minutes, which was about forty-five minutes under the cutoff. That set the tone for the day. With a slower swim, we would have been in trouble. The torrid pace gave us a bit of a cushion, which we needed, as we struggled at times during the bike portion.

When we came in to transition, the crowd was going crazy as we ran up the helix. They were screaming encouragement, and we were feeding off their energy. I let out a big scream and had an ear-to-ear smile on my face.

The bike was one of the biggest hurdles for both of us, as the two of us coupled with the bike weighed about 375 pounds. I wasn't very strong student in physics class, but even I know that was a lot of weight to move over a long distance for an extended time (W x T = D). The first mile of the bike got us really motivated because there were people lined up along the course going crazy. I knew I had to stay focused, as we had a big job ahead of us. I needed to be there for my brother. We weren't here to simply experience the day. We were here to become Ironmen and to prove to anyone who witnessed our feat that anything is possible. Brent and I truly do not feel that this is for us. The glory is great, the media and the notoriety very flattering, but we both believe with every strand of our fiber that this is more for those around us than it is for us. If one person who witnessed this day decides to achieve a goal they didn't think was possible, then it was worth it. There was more riding on our success than a medal or a victory wreath. There was the desire to exhibit proof that anything is possible.

Throughout the 112-mile ride, we averaged just under twelve-and-a-half miles per hour and topped out at forty-one miles per hour. My body felt great, but like all the other athletes out there, I was wiped by the end of our nine-hour ride. It is not a normal position for me, unlike my wheelchair, which is perfectly contoured to my needs and feels like... well, home. The day was a challenge, but the adrenaline, coupled with Brent's positive outlook, really carried us home.

The two-loop bike course offers some incredible views of cow farms and beautiful rolling country roads, but there are three big climbs, affectionately called The Three Sisters. The second of the three, Timberlane

Road, is a tour-like part (as in Tour de France). People line the roads after being bussed out on the course. They scream their heads off and bang on instruments, willing each competitor up the hill. As we climbed the first time, I just kept thinking of the little engine that could. Brent had outfitted me with a bike computer, and I watched our speed drop down from fifteen to nine, to six, and eventually to three miles per hour. I was straining myself. The bike creaked up the hill, I leaned in, yelled, and cheered. As we crested the hill, a man with a drum said, "I will see you on lap two." WAIT...again? Brent told me about the two loops. I knew it, but in my own race, I was intently focused on just one hill. Not unlike every day with CP, I can only control so much, and I focus on each moment.

On the second loop, the crowds were far sparser than the first. Most of the crowd had moved back to town to watch the marathon. We had 375 pounds of human and steel to navigate through the day, and that just meant a slower time than most. As we came upon Timberlane Road, the man with the drum was still there. He walked next to us, banging that drum the entire way up. As we neared the top, exhausted, we realized we had one more climb to go. It was there that we saw Matthew and Erica, waiting to get us up one more hill. Matthew, in his perfectly calm coach speak, told us to get through this one. He told us to work together and lean on each other. He said, "After you recover, it's time to finish this thing." As Brent recovered, I asked, "Hey Bud, we got this?" He gruffly replied, "Yeah." It was time to do this together.

At about mile ninety, we got a little nervous about the time, as we had to finish before 5:30 PM. From this point on, I kept shouting, "We gotta go. We gotta go. I think I can...I think I can." Though our cushion was dwindling, we kept pushing harder until we had nothing left in the tank.

We were one of the last teams to make it before the cutoff, so the fans were extra enthusiastic cheering us to the finish. Those who didn't make the cutoff were done for the day and had to pack up without having a chance to complete their IRONMAN dream. By making the cutoff, we had the pleasure of another five hours on the course, and could keep our dream alive.

Upon the completion of the bike, we went to the transition area, where we did a very quick change. We got our final instructions once again from Coach Rose to make sure we knew what we needed to do to finish this successfully. It's important not to confuse efforts with results. No one remembers those who were almost Ironmen. We were off, and came out to a huge ovation. People were going crazy, and there were cameras going off like a Hollywood premiere.

Toward the end of the race, we went through and around Camp Randall Stadium at the University of Wisconsin, which was one of the highlights of the day. It was dark outside now, and though the stadium was not filled with people, the lights were on and it had a *Chariots of Fire* feel. We had a bike escort, and it was very quiet. Brent and I talked to each other and kept the conversation very light. I was able to get my thoughts together, and it was very peaceful to be there with just Brent. This allowed us to mentally prepare before we reached the big crowds.

At one point, as we exited a crowded area with shops and restaurants, someone shouted out that people we had never met were rooting us on. This has stuck with me to this very day. I love being out there. I love the finishing chute of IRONMAN and sharing that with Brent. But courage and tenacity are traits that people see and identify with. I was given a big boost from that comment and could not wait to find the finish. At around mile twenty-two, one of the volunteers asked to take our photo. At this point, I came to the realization that I was going to be an IRONMAN with my brother. That was the most special part about being an IRONMAN, not by myself, but with Brent. As we were coming to the end, I visualized the chute, just as Coach Rose had taught us from the beginning of our training.

As we neared the finish line at about 10:15 at night, people came out of their houses and onto their porches to clap. With each additional step, the crowd began to swell and explode with enthusiasm. They respected us and they really kept us going.

As we ran up the chute, we saw Mom and gave her a kiss, and then about 350 feet further up the chute, we saw everybody else. I felt like a pitcher who was standing on the mound in the ninth inning of game seven of the World Series, about to see his lifelong dream come true.

About twenty-five feet from the finish, Brent stopped and embraced Erica, and I just screamed. It was one of the happiest days of my life. At that moment, I heard the greatest words I've ever heard: "Kyle and Brent Pease from Atlanta, Georgia...You are an IRONMAN."

Following our accomplishment, I received an email from my father. The feeling that you did something that made your parents visibly proud is one of the greatest feelings I could ever experience:

> Kyle, I usually do not get excited about a trip, a vacation, or other special events until the night before. Then, these special events usually fade a bit a few days after they have ended. Your accomplishment with Brent, becoming an IRONMAN, got me excited with anticipation and beaming with pride at least five days prior to the event. Since then, I have continued to bask in the afterglow. My heart and soul are awash with warm feelings of the strength and brotherly love between you, Brent, and Evan, as well.

> Words do not express my feelings of pride being your father. You have all accomplished so much already in your young lives. You have grown into incredibly good human beings. Thank you for being who you each are, have become, and hope to be in the future. You give hope to so many more who you do not even know.

> There was something else that struck me more than previous races or other events that you and your brothers have been involved in together. That is love. The love that you show for each other in all that you do transcends everything else. It is just beautiful.

CHAPTER 14

EVERY DAY IS AN IRONMAN FOR ME

KYLE

"The Hoyts have paved the way for people like Brent and me. To be a part of that history is amazing. It really is an accomplishment and a credit to the love that me and Brent have for one another."

- KYLE PEASE

No one would have ever believed that IRONMAN Panama City Florida would be accomplished in weather nearly thirty degrees colder than our first IRONMAN in Madison, Wisconsin. Sure, it was November, but no one expected forty-degree temperatures with brisk winds coming off the Gulf of Mexico. Speedos and suntan lotion were replaced by winter hats, mittens, and long sleeves, not only for the spectators but for the athletes as well. I heard one spectator joke that they'd spotted a penguin at the sight of a black and white seagull.

We were extremely excited to take on IRONMAN Panama City. Known as a fast and relatively flat course, we felt that with two IRONMAN finishes on our resume, the IRONMAN officials would almost have to give us entry into Kona. Brent and I arrived on Wednesday, while the crew loaded up the RV on Friday evening, October 31, right after their kids finished trick-or-treating, and made a late-night cannonball run down to the Florida Panhandle. Not much unlike several booze-filled trips to the same location during college, these boys were coming in hot. Their arrival included a tad bit less partying, but the same intensity and energy that always accompanied a trip to Panama City. The crew rolled onto Front Beach Road in Panama City at around 4:30 that morning, following an all-night drive during which none of them were able to catch much sleep. We're told that the seven-hour trip was filled with story-telling, laughter, and a healthy dose of farting from all ends of the RV. They traveled many miles with the windows open to keep awake, but also to keep from being asphyxiated. It takes a village, and this is a one-of-a-kind village that we roll with.

The band from Wisconsin was back together, and though we were ready to take on another challenge, on paper, this one appeared much more manageable than what Wisconsin had thrown at us. Boy, were we wrong. Panama City taught us, in a hurry, to never take anything for granted and to always show respect to the IRONMAN course. It felt like this would be our coronation. No team since the Hoyts had finished multiple IRONMAN competitions, and we were poised to take on number two.

We started setting up our equipment shortly after our arrival, pumping up tires and inflating the kayak in preparation for a successful competition. Brent and I joined three thousand other IRONMAN competitors shortly after six that morning, as we faced the challenge of thirty mile an hour headwinds and dangerous rip-tide currents. My motto is that every day is an IRONMAN for me, and that's what made this event like another day at the office.

We got down to the water early in anticipation of braving the fierce current that strangled the Gulf of Mexico. John David secured my life jacket as the wind continued to whip off the water. I was extremely nervous as the waves pounded against the white beach sand. Because of the rough conditions, IRONMAN had given us an escort swimmer to swim alongside the kayak in case the waves caused me to capsize. The escort was our dear friend Betty Janelle, which made me feel as safe as I possibly could under the circumstances. Having tested the kayak multiple times with Brent, we knew there was only about twenty to thirty seconds to get to me in the event of an incident before I went under. As the crashing waves grew larger by the shore, my mom walked over and told Betty, "Please protect my boys." Betty and my mom both were fighting back tears, knowing that we were about to swim into the teeth of danger.

I looked out at the waves, cresting as white caps against the morning sky. I began to engage in a round of self-talk to convince myself that everything was going to be okay: *We are here to compete, and I'm being protected by my brother and our dear friend Betty. Everything will be fine if I have faith and trust.*

The crowd became restless as the start of the race was delayed several times while race officials tried to determine when or if the weather conditions were likely to improve. I looked over at Brent, and he was like a baseball pitcher waiting to face someone in the bottom of the ninth. He stood silently, staring at the waves with a look of intensity on his face. My brother gets quite intense when racing. He is not the normal protector I am with on so many other occasions. It's both fun and wild to experience that with him. Sometimes I must remind him to smile and appreciate the experience, but in this moment, I looked on and felt the calm finally settling over me. If my starting pitcher could face those waves, so too could I. Brent and I listened for updates, and even heard some chatter about what race organizers would do. Would the race go on or be delayed, or would they just move the swim like they had in St Anthony's all those years ago? We all awaited the sounding of the starter's horn to get a definitive answer, when it was suddenly announced that race organizers had made the decision to change plans and cancel the swim all together. Both my mom and Betty breathed huge sighs of relief, while the crowd of IRONMAN competitors turned their backs to the surf and headed to the bike start.

I was a little disappointed that we would not be able to take on the entire challenge, but as the anxiety subsided and we took stock of what was happening, I admitted to myself that those were some mighty big waves. I am not sure how Brent would have even gotten the boat over some of those without dumping me into the Florida Straits. Watching the lifeguards paddling in their boats, struggling out on the white-capped surf, allowed us to accept the fact that IRONMAN did the right thing in shortening the race. We are always all about safety, and their decision certainly didn't subtract from the experience of the day.

The competition began an hour later than expected, and IRONMAN officials declared the event a duathlon, reducing the length to 138.4 miles. We changed quickly from our wetsuits and had the kayak deflated by some of our crew members so that it wouldn't blow into the Gulf never to be seen or heard from again. Brent and I warmed up a bit in the transition area, changed into some cold weather gear, and pedaled into the teeth of a thirty mile per hour headwind.

As we got ready for the race to start, I realized I had to pee. I did what I always do during races and just let it go. Brent looked over at me in horror and screamed, "What are you doing?" I told him that I had to go and figured I would do what I always did. He said, "It's thirty-nine degrees out and the wind is ripping through our clothes. We have time, man. We should have taken you inside." Brent has lived with me long enough to know how long it would've taken to remove the extra layers and get me into a comfortable position to urinate. Before I could remind him of that, he had toe warmers in his hands and was sticking them to my skin near my hips. My pants were wet, and though I appreciate what he was trying to do, my skin was so burned by the end of the race that it was bubbling. I guess he forgot how warm toe warmers can get when placed against bare skin for fifteen hours.

It was one of the most difficult rides we'd ever experienced, and though the course was relatively flat, we felt that we were riding uphill for each of the 112 miles. Our bike sits up much higher than most, and is, of course, many times heavier than the average racing bike. For much of the race, the headwinds were brutal, seemingly pushing us backwards at times. We were like a captain and his first mate trying to sail against the wind. The first ten miles of the event took us just over an hour, where it would normally take about forty minutes.

How would we ever finish this? The race started like a time trial. With our bib being #122, we were one of the first to go off. Barely pushing double digits on our speedometer meant that more than 2,900 competitors were likely to pass us throughout the day. I don't care who you are; that is mind-numbing and demoralizing. It causes you to question your ability and whether you even care to continue. The wind made the race like a fifteen-round fight for Brent and me. It is normally me that must pull us over the mental hurdles of an IRONMAN whenever Brent begins to struggle. For most of this leg, Brent was coaching me and attempting to keep me focused and positive.

Around mile sixty-two, that began to change. It became evident to me that Brent was breaking down after close to five hours in the saddle. We felt that we could average about thirteen-and-a-half to fourteen miles per hour. It would be a shorter trip than Madison, and we would likely get our long-awaited shot at Kona.

At mile sixty-two, Brent stopped and went off to the bathroom. My skin was burning, my face was whipped from the wind, and my hands were shaking on the handlebars. Brent couldn't see my struggles though, as the toe warmers were below my clothes, my face was pointed forward, rather than back at him, and my arms were strapped down behind heavy Velcro and tape to help my spasms. I wasn't about to tell my brother about it. I was going to fight this by myself without concerning him. I only wanted him to feel my love and feel our spirit push us forward.

As he exited the bathroom, he looked defeated. He told me that he wasn't sure if we could go on, and that this was beyond what either of us expected. I looked down at my odometer and asked him if he could just try biking to mile sixty-three. "Just go one mile, Brent and then we can stop if we need to." He agreed and away we went. At sixty-three, I asked him to just get to mile sixty-four. I was in charge, and any fears

I had, any anxiety about finishing, were gone. My brother needed me, and we were going to do this...TOGETHER. Mile seventy, seventy-one, eighty-five, eighty-six, ninety, ninety-one? "Can you keep going, Bud?" I calmly asked Brent to keep going for one more mile, and he obliged. I looked down at the odometer again as it slowly ticked off each subsequent mile. I begged. I barked. I pushed my brother forward one mile at a time. I so wished I could have miraculously pushed those pedals for him, but moral support was the best I could offer to him. He was grunting, barely speaking, and in so much pain. "Hold my hand, brother. I will get you there. Please, Brent. You got this." For fifty miles, I quite literally counted each mile. I shivered beneath my jacket, I ignored my burning skin and squinted through the howling wind to get Brent to go for just one mile. Every day is an IRONMAN for me, each day I take just one moment at a time. We were doing this, come hell or high water.

BRENT

I couldn't go any longer. It took more than five hours to get through sixty miles. The math wasn't adding up to a successful completion, and I was beat up. I was pushing the pedals harder than I'd expected. We've continued to learn that, no matter the course, no matter the conditions, you get challenged every time. When I went into the woods, I thought about just laying down. Someone would find us eventually and help us get warm, get us good food, and take us home. When I saw Kyle though, I knew. I just knew we had to try. He quietly just asked me for a little more. For nearly four hours, he worked me off the ledge and helped me find a way. Somehow, we kept on trekking along and made the cutoff. Together, we wheel.

Greg Smith was an absolute champ for us on the course, as well, and supplied us with enough laughter to keep things light. We would turn corners onto empty roads and there was Greg, cheering us on with a cowbell, his cell phone camera, and an energy drink. He carried us for many miles when we were nearly ready to throw in the towel.

In some ways, we have a competitive advantage because we are with each other the whole time and we can talk each other through challenges like this. I think it works both ways. I can't do this without Brent, and Brent can't do this without me, so I think, when we work together, we get the best outcome. It's not always easy, but the challenge helps us to see what we are both capable of. I am as proud of that bike ride as any we have ever completed.

We got off the bike and I was frozen solid. While Brent refueled, I laid on the ground in the transition area tent, trying to thaw out and regain focus. Thankfully, the transition changing area was indoors. We were able to warm up, get dry clothes on, and regroup for the marathon. The sun set quickly on us, and with it came even colder temperatures. A two-loop run meant that we had to see the finish line, only to turn away from it for a second lap. This was my turn to want to wave the white flag. My butt was hurting, my legs were tight, my skin was burned, and my face was chapped, raw, and red from the constant wind slapping my cheeks all day long.

There is one part of the course that is in a protected park, so no one is allowed there except runners. There is not even an aid station on that section of the course. It was so dark during that stretch that we could barely see in front of us. On the other hand, it was so quiet and peaceful that I could hear Brent breathing while his feet hit the pavement in rhythm. The click of the wheels acted like a metronome keeping the beat of the music. It was an oddly special moment that I will remember forever. Amidst the suffering, the cold, and the sheer distance of the day, we were out here again together, two brothers enjoying what we love most. I forgot about my pain, refocused on the mission at hand, and started pushing Brent forward even harder. We were passing many of the folks that had passed us earlier in the day. We were showing them that we weren't just people to clap for, but a force to be reckoned with.

We ran by our family, all bundled up from the cold. We stopped briefly and exchanged hugs and high-fives; there were steady streams of tears on all their faces. We saw the race director, Ben, who ran with us for a while, and with tears in his eyes, thanked us for being a part of the race. You meet so many amazing people in this sport, in this life, and Ben was an individual who positively impacted us, and stuck with us long after the finish of the event. Never had we encountered someone who worked so hard to provide us with a positive experience.

We completed the marathon with a time of 4:28:15, our fastest IRONMAN run to that point, and finished the slightly shortened IRONMAN with a time of 13:53:08. As always, we crossed the finish line, not with me in front of Brent, but symbolically side-by-side, to the sound of the announcer's voice echoing our favorite words in the entire language: "Kyle Pease...Brent Pease...You are an IRONMAN."

CHAPTER 15

IF WE CAN MAKE IT THERE, WE CAN MAKE IT ANYWHERE

KYLE AND BRENT

"Predestined conditions don't ever dictate the outcome of the final chapter."

- KYLE PEASE

More families arrived throughout the course of the week, and by race day, we had more than seventy family members, fans, and spectators there to root us on. Hopefully they'd witness something that had only happened twice before, and obviously never involved us. We knew that when we were out there, we were not going to be representing just ourselves, our families, and our loved ones—we would also be representing The Kyle Pease Foundation and all the families we support. That's why we're doing this, to support them, and show them that anything is possible.

In addition, the love that Brent and I share for each other is genuine and heartfelt. What we accomplish together is the result of the strong bond and *commitment we have for one another. To accomplish this together, on the largest stage in the world, is a testament to love, togetherness, and family. The lack of each is a huge issue in the world today, and though we in no way believe that competing in a race together will change the world, we do feel that if we inspire one family, one set of brothers or sisters, to become a little bit closer, than we will have accomplished a wonderful blessing through our efforts.*

KYLE

By 2015, the foundation was growing by leaps and bounds. We no longer raced with only eight people at Publix, but instead with nearly twenty. A local 5K brought about a dozen athletes every weekend. It was starting to grow bigger than me, bigger than either of us. As much as I loved a local 5K, I still loved doing one race with just my brother. Enter the New York City Marathon.

We had first approached the race organizers in 2011 to see if we could enter the race. Despite accepting nearly 52,000 other athletes, we were shot down because of their rule that you must be able to finish under your own power. Each year, we would try and convince race officials to make an exception to the rule, and each year their response was the same. In 2014, things started to change a bit. Brent flew to NYC and met with some of the leadership. They promised us that they were looking into it and were working on establishing ways to include all runners. Sometime after IRONMAN Florida, they informed us that there would be a lottery to accept five athletes as a test case to see how to manage this style of racing. Brent and I entered our names into the lottery, crossed our fingers, said prayers, and hoped for the best.

As luck would have it, our name was pulled. Brent and I would head to the Big Apple to share the streets of Brooklyn, Manhattan, Queens,

Staten Island, and the Bronx with over 50,000 other runners. Perhaps our luck ended there, or perhaps it was just beginning.

As we prepared for the race, there was another very momentous event in the Pease family, as Brent and Erica welcomed their first child, a beautiful redheaded girl named Caroline, into the world. It was so special to see this tiny human enter our world, with her whole life in front of her. I worried if she would love me and wondered if she would treat me like Brent does. I knew from the moment that I laid eyes on her that Uncle Kyle was going to spoil her rotten.

BRENT

In one monumental three-week period, Kyle Pease Foundation athletes competed in the Marine Corps Marathon, NYC Marathon, and IMFL. First up was Marine Corps. We had a new truck, generously donated by a great supporter, to help haul equipment to the nation's capital. We didn't have to rent a truck, and we were so excited to experience the growth of the foundation. On the way home from DC, disaster struck. The gas pedal wasn't responding, and I had to pull off into a truck stop. Thankfully, they had a repair center, but in a cruel twist of fate, they didn't have the required part. After two full days of eating truck stop lunch buffets and sleeping in a less-than-glamorous truck stop motel, the part arrived, and they finally had me back on the road.

My wife was ever-patient to see me return to our new baby girl, Caroline, but I was coming back for barely a full day before we were off to NYC. I was missing the opportunity to spend time with my growing family, but after four years of fighting for this opportunity with Kyle, we whisked off to the Big Apple. Our streak of bad luck should have been over, I thought, as we headed north to compete in the largest marathon in the world and share another 26.2 miles together. We really had no expectations or lofty goals other than to enjoy the race and experience

New York City. Our first thirteen miles was an incredible experience. I'm not sure what our time was, because honestly, that's not what this race was about. We were enjoying the crowd, the sights, sounds, and smells of this incredible metropolis, and most importantly, an anticipated three-and-a-half hour run with each other.

After roughly thirteen miles, our luck would change again. Our wheel started making noise at around mile eight. Kyle asked if we were okay and I responded, "Yes." It was the same affirmative answer I gave him in 2010, when he asked if people in wheelchairs could do IRONMAN. Of course, athletes in wheelchairs could finish the NYC Marathon, I thought. The news got worse and worse, seemingly with each rotation of the wheel. I shouted out a long string of unrepeatable expletives, and then I really started to get upset. And then it happened.

I peeked down at the back-left wheel, and there were three broken spokes. One broken spoke in a chair of this construction is bad. Three broken spokes is catastrophic. With the next step we took, the wheel disintegrated into a nearly unrecognizable pile of broken metal. I ripped Kyle from the chair and hoisted him next to my chest, the same way I had carried him down the twenty-seven stairs nearly twenty-six years earlier to play in our living room. I made the decision that I was going to carry my 110-pound brother in my tired arms for the next thirteen miles. *He ain't heavy, he's my brother*, I thought. That was just male bravado kicking in. We barely made it 500 feet. I stopped, and the crowd of onlookers curiously wondered aloud what was happening and how long it was going to take me to realize that my attempt to continue was futile. I asked for help—no, I begged for help, and some kind strangers left the sidewalk and carried Kyle's mangled wheelchair, while I carried Kyle to the medical tent. I explained to the staff what had occurred, as my concern was that they would look at Kyle's permanently contorted body and assume that he, rather than his chair, required medical attention. We laid Kyle on a cot and I took out my phone and began making calls to whomever popped into my head. I called Erica, then Coach Matthew, then Greg, before texting Betty.

Matthew told me calmly that we had nothing to prove, that it was not us quitting. It just wasn't our day. I told him we just wanted to check all options. We couldn't live with walking off the course at the halfway point if we didn't at least try. This was simply who we were, and this was part of the lesson that Kyle had taught us since entering the world thirty years ago. A quote from Henry Ford entered my exhausted brain and seemed to give me all the motivation that we would need: "There is no disgrace in honest failure; there is disgrace in fearing to fail."

We grabbed a couple of NYC cops and shared our dilemma. They helped us to take the chair to a bike shop nearby. The bike mechanics looked at the wheel and told me they could have it back in one to two days. I chuckled, wiped the sweat from my brow and pointed to my bib. "I am in the race. We were hoping to get back out there much sooner than one to two days." Then I had an idea. They cut the mangled wheel off the chair, and I headed back to the medical tent.

Upon my arrival, I saw some medical personnel, our brother Evan, who had been watching the race, and a race official all conversing. Kyle had been there long enough that they were trying to present us with the paperwork to drop out. I begged for two more minutes and asked the staff to help me execute my final attempt to complete the race. Together, we fashioned some rope and a few blankets, and tied the chair to my shoulder. We just had to try. I knew that's what Kyle would do. I knew what he did his entire life: He never gave up. He always tried to find a way to keep moving forward.

We placed Kyle back into the chair and attempted to reenter the race. Once again, we were not racing for time, as that was long out the window. We were now racing for principle. The slightly reconstructed race chair wasn't performing well. You must put pressure on the back of the chair in order to turn it, lifting the front wheel slightly off the ground and twisting the chair in the direction you want to go. With the missing wheel, I couldn't balance, lift, and turn the chair. A woman running by offered her assistance. We both stubbornly grunted no. She insisted and told us we needed help. We relented, and Amy from Baltimore became our "third wheel." This was a totally selfless act, as she forfeited her own personal marathon time in order to help a couple of strangers. Amy began turning the chair for us. We were going to do this. Her efforts kept twisting the front wheel, causing the chair to dig into my shoulder. I could feel the chaffing starting as the rope was burning my skin. We had her take the broken side of the chair in the back and literally help me shoulder the load.

Around mile sixteen, another runner, Kamran from NYC, came along and grabbed the chair. At that point all three of us were tired, so we didn't mind the extra set of hands. We now had a four-person team. Kyle smiled graciously and talked to our newfound friends. As difficult as this was, even with four of us, we needed Kyle to encourage us all to keep going.

Mentally, I was really struggling. We weren't doing this on our own. This wasn't us and wasn't what we stood for. I didn't want to keep going. At mile eighteen, I asked everyone to leave. I pushed the chair to the curb and told Kyle that this was pointless, that there was no reason to continue. I told him we could always try again next year. He looked at me with fire in his eyes and told me that I could quit, but that he was going to finish, somehow, some way. Kyle was willing to break up the team of brothers and continue the race without me. He may not have seen it through his irrational emotions, but that was what I needed to hear. There was no way I was going to leave him to cross the finish line without me, yet I had no idea. It was so tough at this point. The rope snapped so I was switching hands every few feet to take pressure off my arms. Amy and Kamran took turns holding sides and helping to turn the chair. We were having some genuine brotherly moments, and not always the good kind. We were being human, being brothers, and just trying to find a way.

Around mile twenty-three, I just stopped talking. I was angry that Kyle would make me stay out there, blaming him for my emotions. I was making it all about me. I was reacting to what was happening and not sharing that with Kyle. He sensed it. He knew it. What was on pace to be a 3:25 minute day was pushing well past seven hours on the course. We were grinding out twenty-two-minute miles, when, under normal conditions, our pace is about three times as fast.

Little did we know what was happening in Atlanta, as people were going nuts on social media. They could see this unfolding all over the internet in real time, and the cheers were coming from all over the country. Maybe that's what kept me going. Maybe it was the lesson I could share with my daughter one day, or maybe I just wanted to give Kyle the strength he tried so hard to give me. What I heard from him at mile eighteen taught me that no matter how rough it got, I had to keep going. Together, with total strangers helping us, we found a way. After seven hours and thirty-two minutes, we finally found the finish. Our motto, "Where There's a Wheel, There's a Way," was replaced by a similar sentiment: "Where There's Not a Wheel, There's Still a Way." Race officials brought us a spare wheelchair, and whisked Kamran and Amy away. We shouted to them to keep in touch. Amy was crying, and Kamran had the biggest smile on his face. They could have finished hours before, but they'd stopped for us, a true gesture of generosity and chivalry.

As we walked towards Kyle's chair, I pulled out my phone. Unbeknownst to me, my phone had been going nuts the entire five hours since the wheel broke. I called Erica, and tears started flowing from both ends of the phone line. I couldn't talk. She told me how proud she was of both me and of Kyle. I blubbered, "I love you," through my tears and thanked her for taking care of our family and for giving me this opportunity. She told me she was tired, too, and asked me to hurry home.

I called Betty and shed more tears as she told me that we just gave so many the greatest gift we could ever share; that by not giving up, we showed Atlanta and the rest of the world what was possible with the mind. As we slumped into the cab, I shared with Kyle what had happened while we were out there. I told him that I know it got hard and got negative, but we didn't give up. I told him how proud people were and how moved they were. Instead of embracing me and forgiving me for my behavior, he started shouting at me. He told me how bad I was out there, and that I didn't give it my all. I shouted back. I cursed. I told him he could just get himself home. I was hurt that this was how he would respond, but he was right. There is no quitting in Kyle's life, no matter how difficult things get. He has likely wanted to "leave it by the side of the road" many times, and that is simply not an option. Find a way, figure it out; quitting is not a word in the daily life of Kyle Pease.

When we got back to the hotel, we both realized that I still had to help him brush his teeth, to go to the bathroom, and to go to bed. We both silently wished the other one would just leave. We were still mad at each other, yet we needed each other. No matter how bad things get, we were still brothers, through thick and thin. We silently got ready for bed and turned off the lights.

When we woke up, Kyle was much calmer. We just hugged and offered each other a silent apology, a silent I love you. When he was ready, I showed him his phone, and he couldn't believe it. We were suddenly inundated with interview requests from major media outlets up and down the East Coast. We were flooded with messages as total strangers began reaching out and thanking him for his courage. It finally set in for Kyle that even at our worst, we can still let our best shine through. On the ride to the airport, we started talking again. I told him how proud I was and thanked him for not letting me quit at mile eighteen. I thanked him for being my brother, and he muttered the same before laughing and saying it again with conviction.

We kept in touch with Amy and Kamran and have since learned that Amy has two sons with special needs. They have run races with us since then, which was extra special to us all. Kyle and I learned to share the sordid details of our toughest day together. The one where it wasn't perfect, but we still found a way. Nobody wants a DNF, and I am so glad we didn't get one on this day. I am so proud of our team and what we can do when we do it together.

ERICA

I was in the kitchen with our newborn daughter, Caroline, when Brent called. He seemed very calm when he told me that the racing chair had broken and they were unable to finish. He didn't necessarily sound defeated, but I could tell he was trying to process what had happened. He told me he'd tried to carry Kyle but was unable to make it more than a few hundred yards. They'd visited an aid station, looking for assistance, with the only solution to jimmy it up to his shoulder. He knew this wasn't going to work, but he wasn't ready to give up on Kyle.

Brent called me back when he had a real solution, sounding relieved. I spent the afternoon glued to my phone as I watched the mile tracker approach twenty-six miles. My phone rang off the hook, as all our friends were going crazy watching. No one could believe that, after seven hours, they did it. They had accomplished the unthinkable.

It was that day that I realized this whole thing, the KPF, is much bigger than Brent and Kyle. Their message resonates with people because everyone truly wants to have hope. Brent and Kyle gave that to us that day and showed us how something as small as a seven-hour walk can make such an impact on the community.

CHAPTER 16

IRONMAN BOULDER:
FAILING TO PREPARE IS PREPARING TO FAIL

BRENT

*"If you believe in something and you want to do it, go after it.
Don't let anything stop you from what you want to do in life."*

- KYLE PEASE

By Thursday, though I began to get excited as more and more friends and family arrived, I wanted to remain calm and focused on what we were about to battle. The island itself has a relatively small population during most times of the year, but during IRONMAN time, the population temporarily explodes. The island had a different feel than any other race we had ever competed in. This was the IRONMAN World Championship, and I couldn't pull the smile from my face the entire week at the realization that I was actually here.

We were invited to appear with Bob Babbitt on his talk show, Breakfast with Bob. The show took place on the beach, and I was unable to get down *there in my wheelchair. So, Brent carried me down and had to prop me up on the couch next to him so I didn't tip over during the interview. Once again, this isn't a good look for a potential IRONMAN, but is indicative of some of the challenges I must deal with that other competitors do not.*

Bob is one of those people who really makes you feel good about yourself. You feel like you want to want to hang out with him all the time. He is like the grandfather of IRONMAN, so to be in his presence feels like you are with royalty. He asked us a lot of different questions about the race and how we felt, and even asked us about the Hoyts and how it felt follow in their footsteps. Bob made me feel extremely comfortable. It didn't feel like an interview, but more like a couple of guys sitting around a table and talking IRONMAN.

The sole reason we went to Boulder, Colorado, to compete in our third IRONMAN is because Kyle and I had created something that we enjoyed doing. We had been trying to break through and earn an invitation to Kona for three years, and it felt like we were never going to get in. We had battled the hills of Wisconsin, the cold of Florida, the equipment malfunction in New York, and still couldn't get a sniff of the yellow hibiscus of the Hawaiian Islands. So, we thought, let's just do a race. No expectations, no ulterior motive, just 140.6 grueling miles between brothers. We loved being athletes together, so decided to go have some fun.

The only races available to teams like ours were Wisconsin and Boulder, and since we had already done Wisconsin, Boulder was the obvious choice. The race was on a Saturday and we got there on Wednesday. We had been away from a full IRONMAN for three years. Arriving in Boulder a few days before the race with Erica, Caroline, Kyle, and our skeleton crew, which consisted of Dad and our friend Jason, a former Marine and Atlanta SWAT officer who was just the right calm we needed in our corner. He was the one that held us all in control! It allowed us time to adjust to the altitude. Prior to the flight, Kyle drank quite a bit of water to help with his level of hydration. He began to feel a bout of diarrhea coming on while on the flight, and had to visit the bathroom with his good friend and caretaker for this race, Ian. Knowing the miniscule size of an airplane bathroom, it is difficult to envision two fully grown men trying to navigate such tight quarters. Another challenge in the life of Kyle that most of us simply take for granted.

We had an opportunity to do a short video with IRONMAN while in town and get our story in front of the audience in Boulder. Boulder is kind of the mecca of triathlon states, at least in the lower forty-eight, so a ton of triathletes reside in the area. Our whole reason for being there was to enjoy ourselves, and that is exactly what we did. On Friday, we got to meet Australian IRONMAN Mirinda Carfrae. Her reputation precedes her in the sport of triathlon. Kyle was even a bit awestruck at the chance to talk with "Rinny."

The race began, and we had an amazing swim, completing it in one hour and seven minutes, our fastest yet. We flew through transition with the help of our pit crew, Dad and Jason. We got to experience a three-loop bike course, which we had never done before, and everything was going flawlessly. I said to Kyle that, even though it was still an IRONMAN, the fact that we were competing with no pressure and no predetermined expectations made it a very relaxed and enjoyable experience. We got to see spectators and family and friends who were there with us. They all came out to enjoy it as well, and it became like one big, hard-fought party. We did the first loop in about two-and-a-half hours. We thought, *Holy crap, we're flying. We're going to breeze through this day.*

Then, the wheels slowly started coming off. At around the halfway point, Kyle pooped his pants, but he refused to stop. In his head, we had to keep going or we risked not making the bike cutoff; both Wisconsin and Florida had been dramatic, as we made the cutoffs with not much time to spare.

I started coming apart as we began the third lap. Part of it was the altitude starting to get to me. My heart rate was high all day, making it harder to eat. I was also having a little trouble breathing, which might have been allergies. Either way, we were both really starting to struggle. At that point, most of our supporters had gone. The course was getting empty and we'd been out there for a long time. I was running out of energy, as I realized that I hadn't eaten enough. Betty screamed at me, "You gotta eat." I had chips and a Coke in my pocket, so I slowed down enough to take in some calories, and that helped big time.

We hit mile 112, and I was looking for the transition, which was when we learned that the transition was officially at 114, so we had two extra miles to ride. We hit transition and I just handed the bike to my dad and Jason and walked away. I was so gassed that I hardly realized I'd left Kyle behind.

We went into the tent for more than twenty minutes. I was laying down, trying to get some salt and attempting to fix my body. Kyle was hiding behind towels and also trying to fix his body—he was chafed and rubbed raw from sitting in his own fecal matter for four-plus hours. It was a good reminder of how difficult the sport is. It doesn't matter how fit we are or how strong we are, each race presents challenges. Wisconsin was all hills and sheer volume. Florida was the wind and the cold. In Boulder, it turned out to be the altitude and distance while Kyle struggled with some physical issues. All the challenges made each experience good for us, and getting through them all provided us with valuable lessons we would need for Kona.

We finally set out on the run, and Kyle was struggling so much that we had to keep stopping. We'd pull into an aid station, and I'd ask a volunteer to give him some chips, Gatorade, and Coke. I'd then go grab everything I needed, because I hadn't eaten for hours and my stomach was nearly empty. We'd get back out there and slowly chip away at this thing, making up some of the time we had lost during the ride and the lengthy transition. It was a beautiful run, a path lined with people all along a creek.

The finish line was one of the bigger celebrations because we had one of our larger groups cheering us on. We stopped and high-fived everybody because we were so damn happy. We'd gotten through one of the harder race experiences we'd had in an IRONMAN together. We finished Boulder in about 15:04, faster than Wisconsin. Florida was faster than Boulder, but the swim had been cancelled. It wasn't the course that got us, but just the race itself. While we were stronger than we had been during our previous attempts, we still needed a strong reminder how challenging it is to race 140.6 miles. While usually reserved and looking quite tired at the end of the race, Kyle is the one who lets out the loudest screams. As we stopped and saw our swim coach, Maria, I let out a scream that was equal in decibel level to that of Kyle's. We had sat in T2 for more than twenty minutes, both of us wondering how our bodies could carry on for a marathon. Yet we'd found a way, once again, to never stop. One wheel, one foot in front of the other, and we got to celebrate one more time in a sport that had given us both so much.

In hindsight, going to Boulder was a phenomenal decision. We would otherwise likely have forgotten some things by the time we got to Kona if it had been four years since our last IRONMAN. When we got to the start line at Kona, we had just done an IRONMAN a year ago, so it was fresh in our minds, and we knew what we had to work on. I practiced my nutrition all summer and increased my training for Kona. I had a plan there, and I didn't have one when we went to Boulder. Failure to prepare is preparing to fail. I certainly took it for granted, thinking that I'd done so many IRONMANs that I knew what I had to do. For Kona, I knew I had to pay attention to those details. Kyle and I practiced everything in order to be ready. All that preparation, what we learned at Boulder, was part of what helped us succeed in Kona.

CHAPTER 17

PRIOR TO TODAY

BRENT

———

"I had 1,500 other things going on other than worrying about Kona. I remember getting to Raleigh and just thinking, 'I'm good. I'll do this race with Kyle, and I'll just take a break the rest of the summer.'"

- BRENT PEASE

To be able to do Kona, you must finish a half or full triathlon in a calendar year. For the last few years, we've always entered a half to make sure we would be qualified, just in case our name was to be called. On top of that, we just enjoy doing them. It's easy to travel and they aren't as expensive. We've been able to see some cool things over the years, from Boulder, Colorado, to Muncie, Indiana, and many places in between. Even though 70.3 miles is a daunting task, it is not nearly as harsh as the more than fifteen hours of racing when taking on 140.6 miles.

There are a lot more people racing this distance, and that sometimes limits our options, but we were happy to find Raleigh available, only six hours from Atlanta and a straight shot up I-85. It's known as a fun race with a beautiful bike course. The timing was perfect, too, so that if we were to somehow get into Kona, we'd have done a race in June and then start prepping for the crown jewel, Kona.

We've learned, since Florida 70.3 in 2017, that it's not all about Kona, but really it is all about Kona. What I mean is that every year, we think about it. We talk about it. We wish on it. We will ourselves to try to get there. Being in Florida, we realized that it was bigger than us. We had all these people who believed in us and supported us. We had people who showed up, forty or fifty or more, at the Publix Marathon each year. People really believe in and are impacted by everything else that has grown from what Kyle and I started, what was once just the two of us, so if Kona never happened, we had to accept it and realize that a lot of good had still come from this seemingly unlikely quest.

Perhaps one of the greatest joys is watching people show what is truly possible. An IRONMAN is hard for anyone but imagine being confined all day to a wheelchair and then teaching your body how to manage 70.3 or 140.6 miles of fun. In 2015, JDude was the first to take on the journey with our support. With the help of some incredible volunteers, he found the finish line of his first IRONMAN. The next year we had athletes racing in Augusta, showing us true courage and finishing despite a flat tire. This past year, it was Jon Crais and Thomas Odom taking on the half distance in Macon, GA. IRONMAN is a true test of endurance and we are honored so many have taken on that challenge and allowed us to play a small part in their journeys.

I went into Raleigh with a little uncertainty, thinking, *I'm not sure I can do this*. Erica and I had just bought a house. We'd added to our family, as little Henry had joined Erica, Caroline, and me. Kyle and I hadn't really had as much time to train together as we would have normally liked to have had liked, and it just didn't feel like Kona was going to happen. In the back of my mind, though, I said, "You love doing these half IRONMANs with your brother, and these half IRONMANs are usually an opportunity to race by yourselves. You don't have to worry about anybody but each other. Enjoy that part of it."

With that carefree attitude in mind, the swim was great. It was beautiful. As much as it takes out of me, I like swimming in that warmer water.

The bike course is in a rural area by Lake Jordan, about forty minutes outside of Raleigh; you do some biking up on the hills around the lake, then hop on a beautiful highway for a stretch before slowly working your way back into "The City of Oaks," Raleigh. Many cyclists and triathletes enjoy training out on this beautiful country course. The first part of the bike ride was just quiet and scenic. We weren't saying much to each other because there really wasn't much to say. Then we started chatting and enjoying it, and we started pushing each other and climbing more hills. Then it got hotter and harder. Then we had a flat tire that we kind of band-aided. We moaned and groaned and pushed and somehow got to the finish line, literally rolling in on the rim. The run was hot and hilly, but as we started heading down, Kyle screamed and yelled, and I tried to keep up with him.

Before we knew it, we crossed the finish line. I didn't think anything of it. I just thought, *This was so much fun, this was wonderful.* I plopped down, in a wheelchair of all places, and just sat there. The announcer, David, kept asking to take a picture, but I just wanted a cold drink. I just wanted some ice and to relax a bit, but he kept pestering us, so I finally got up. There are a lot of people who truly supported us, and David is one them. He really wanted to push our story out there and make people aware of what we are doing. He writes some great content and does announcing for IRONMAN. He enjoys being a part of the sport and meeting people like Kyle and me.

I begrudgingly got up from the chair to appease David and walked over with Kyle to look pretty for the camera. I thought they were just taking a picture. Instead, David grabbed the microphone and his voice boomed through the loudspeaker: "Kyle and Brent, on behalf of IRONMAN, because it's the fortieth anniversary of IRONMAN, we would like to invite you two to race in Kona this year and inspire us for another forty years."

If you watch the video, Kyle looks shocked. It took a second or more for the sound to travel from my ears to my brain so that I could process what I had just heard. I cocked my head slightly, replayed his words in my head...and then the emotion really flowed. I thought of all the struggles, the self-doubt, wondering whether this was the right time or whether we could do it at all, contemplating the fact that it might never happen. Despite the hard moments, we'd stuck with it, just like we do in our races, just like Kyle does every day, and just like what so many other people who run with us as part of the foundation do. It may have been allergies, but I'm pretty sure it was emotions that came pouring out of my eyes, down my cheeks, and on to my sweaty race shirt.

I gave Kyle a hug and held on tight because I knew as soon as I let go, it wouldn't be about us anymore. It would be about everything we had to do to get ready, all the money we would have to raise, and all the people we would need to talk to.

When I looked at Kyle, he was ready to start screaming because he was so damn excited. That was pure. It was raw. It was real. And that was incredible to watch. They even gave us the golden ticket to make the invite official, just like in *Willy Wonka and the Chocolate Factory*.

Anything worthwhile is always worth the struggle. There's usually a struggle attached to it, whether it's just living, or your relationship with your brother, your wife, or your job. There are always going to be ups and downs. I certainly wish we'd had an opportunity to get to Kona before this year, but now I appreciate the struggles we went through to be able to finally get there. It will make us work hard for the opportunity, because we don't know if it will ever happen again.

Every one of these races had its own difficulty. When you think back, when we first did New Orleans, we had eight gears on the bike. It took us almost five hours to do the bike leg, and it was exhausting—but when we talk about New Orleans now, we talk about how cool it was that we finished on eight gears, how great we felt when we finished, and how sunburned Kyle was because we took his jacket off and didn't give him sunscreen. We talk about Wisconsin and how glorious that day was, but those hills were freaking hard. We questioned at times if we could finish. Raleigh was the same. My tough moments were just a function of where I was personally. Yet, when we were finished, it was all worth it in the end.

This time, it was worth it in a different way. The year before, we'd learned that it wasn't just about one race. Kyle and I still brought strong desire to each race, but we didn't live and die by one event alone. It wasn't going to define who we were. We weren't going to let it define us.

Sometimes, the scary part is just finishing the race. In Wisconsin, we were worried about finishing. In Florida, we didn't even think twice about it until the wind picked up. In Boulder, it was briefly a consideration on the bike course when we started to struggle on the third lap, but it was never a big consideration. It wasn't like, "Oh my gosh, we've got to hurry, we're not going to make it." I think that finding things that scare you is a good thing. I think we've found things that will help us grow, and that is part of the journey.

Kona is a scary race. When we raced Boulder in 2017, it was rated as a harder IRONMAN course than Kona, but in Kona you have unbelievable heat. You have wind. You have the trade winds that can blow across, and feel like they're blowing into you all day, and even as you turn around to get back into town, they're somehow still blowing into you. You have a race that's so popular there are even restrictions as to where people can be on the course, and you can spend miles in isolation.

But if your dreams don't scare you, then they're not big enough. And that's why we've always focused on Kona—because it is the biggest thing we can possibly take on. We're battle-tested from our past races, and I like that. We want to make sure that when we show up on October 13, we're ready to give every ounce of energy we have to that race. But there's so much more. 2018 is the year where things start to shift, where we get an opportunity to grow in a way that we never really thought possible.

I would have loved to have been able to do this sooner, to have had this opportunity sooner, but I honestly don't know if we would have been ready in 2012. The struggles along the way made each year special and made us better. The work we're doing has continued to snowball. More and more people are Walking with KPeasey every day. We just had fifty-eight people do one race with us. We had ten people join the Peachtree

Road Race. We had two people join the New York City Marathon. We've sent someone to New York every year since we first did it. Publix was an opportunity for us to do things together, and now we provide that opportunity to so many others. We want people to walk away from Publix and do every race with us. And every year, we have someone who does Publix and doesn't stop racing.

We have so many people behind us. We have the energy of an army of people to walk with, to walk alongside, to carry us across each finish line. These are the people who are cheering us on in our dark moments. With them, because of them, this became our year to be selected, and it feels like everything is in the right place.

Whether or not we made it to Kona wasn't going to affect the foundation's ability to serve. We would have just invested more and more energy into those around us, while still having some fun together, whether that meant doing a Half IRONMAN or a sprint triathlon. We love being out there, struggling all day together and getting through the ups and the downs. We enjoy laughing and having fun, and we enjoy having to pick each other up. We enjoy getting through it and drinking Coke on the run course or chicken broth or chips or hamburgers after. We love ordering a beer after every race and just letting it sit on the table. We ordered a bottle of champagne after Raleigh. Kyle had a sip and I had two sips. One of these days, we'll get through a celebratory drink.

One of the first questions Kyle had asked me about triathlons was if people in wheelchairs could do them. He also asked me what it felt like to do one. I told him, "It's a lot like your life." It's an extreme day of ups and downs. In the pictures from our first one, we're just happy and all smiles. When we get down, it's like the sky is falling. When we see athletes in that dark place, falling apart, it's very relatable. We can also look at them and then at each other and know that we're going to get through it together.

We won't give up. They would have to pick us up off the course, kicking and screaming, because we won't be alone. I look forward to being with my brother as I reach for my "Never quit" bracelet. Or he'll reach back to me and say something or share a story. We finally get the opportunity we've been waiting for since the end of 2012, when we first asked if we could be there in Kona. And this time, they said yes.

I know that we're not defined, nor will we ever be defined, by Kona. People won't look at us and think, "There are the IRONMAN world champs," as much as they say, "Those are the brothers who race together and have a foundation." I think that's more the reality of who we are and how we're perceived. (Kyle, of course, wants to be called Kona Kyle from now on, and he deserves that.) Oftentimes in life, when you're squeezing, things don't happen until you let go. That's what we did. We went to Raleigh, we went to Boulder, to start the process of letting go. Boulder was a great time all week, cutting up just like we were in Wisconsin, telling fart jokes and having a good time. It was a great experience. We went to Raleigh to say, "Hey, let's go and do this. We probably won't get in this year, but let's go do it anyway," and we relaxed. We had a fun time together. Then we got this massive news and had nobody to celebrate with us. Erica was at home, my mom was at home, Betty and all these people who are usually with us were all at home, because it just wasn't a big deal. It was just a small thing we did, just for us.

I didn't have my phone. Erica said she was the last one to find out, but that was not true. She was the first one to find out. I called her, still sobbing. (Yeah, I cry a bit.) There have only been a couple of times in my life when I couldn't get my words to come out. This was one of them. I called her to tell her we were in, and I just couldn't put the words together. And yet, she already knew. That's what makes Erica such a wonderful compliment to what we do. She sacrifices as much or more than Kyle and I do for the cause and always knows what I am thinking and what is happening in my life.

Then I talked to Matthew, and he asked if I was for real, and I said, "Yeah, man. This is real. We're in. We're going to Kona."

By the time I got back to the hotel, we had raised money already. Greg Smith was on the phone fundraising, and we had $38,000 raised, just like that, because there are people that have been with us since the beginning that want to see this through. Even though none of us were squeezing this tight, we want to tighten our grip and see this through.

KONA is a lifetime of looking over the fence and seeing Kyle just waiting and watching as everyone else played on.

KONA is a village of volunteers along for every step of the journey to help us get here.

Kyle is a hero to me as well as to many others, but he is also my brother, the brother who grew up sharing in it all, the good and the bad.

Come October, we get to share one of the greatest challenges yet, and Kyle won't be watching this time. He will be carrying me down to the beach, through the swim, and out into the lava fields to pedal with me all up and down the Queen K. Then, hopefully, we will run till we reach the finisher's chute, where we will hear our name called out as Ironmen.

I am in awe that we will have this opportunity and cannot wait to share it with my brother. This is the culmination of our dreams. Together.

Behind Every Good Man

Erica

I was sitting in the kitchen with Henry in my arms when Brent called. I assumed he was calling to say the race was over and they had finished. I wasn't really tracking what was going on, because it's too hard to with the two kids. The first thing he said was, "We got in. We did it." And I said, "Well, oh great. You finished." He said, "No, we got in. We're going to Hawaii." I was truly just floored. I mean like, blown away. He didn't have any answers and couldn't really explain what had happened. He just kept saying, "We got in. We got in."

We got off the phone and I immediately texted Coach Matthew and Greg Smith, who both called right away and asked, "What do you mean?" I said, "They got in. I don't know how or any more behind it, but they got in."

I've had friends say, "Well, you knew what you were getting yourself into," but I didn't. When Brent and I met in the fall of 2007 and connected permanently in the summer of 2008, he was just doing his first triathlon. It was an Olympic distance in Chattanooga, and I thought, *Oh, that's cute. He did a triathlon.* This was not his life. Then, in 2010, it was like, *Neat, great. Brent and Kyle get to do triathlons together.* Things have changed quite a bit in the past eight to ten years.

When I got that phone call about Kona, that's when the attitude had to shift. I needed to shift my perspective and my expectations of Brent; he'd gone from being a husband and a father and someone who works two full-time jobs outside of our house (the coaching business and the foundation), to an elite athlete in training for the ultimate IRONMAN competition. The priority needed to be on training.

I'm not going to lie, it was not an easy summer. It's hard being around the house with two little kids. Henry was still so little (five months old in June), so I couldn't really do much with him very easily. I relied a lot on all four grandparents and my friends to plan activities, to get me out of the house, and to keep me occupied. A lot of times I had bad anxiety because I knew I was going to be on my own for nine, ten, eleven hours a day with both children. That pretty much was my schedule for the seventeen weeks leading up to the race. We were around the clock with preparations, Brent's travel, speech, and life obligations.

I don't think a lot of people realize the sacrifices our whole family had to make. Richard and Janis sacrificed a lot this summer to help on the weekends. My parents blew it out of the water with the amount of help they gave. They took the kids all nine days that we were out of town, no questions asked.

I had to put my own personal needs to the side, which was okay. I've never had to do that before and I won't have to again for a long time, but it was worth the sacrifices. Brent wrote me a nice letter showing his appreciation for me; I looked at it an opportunity for myself, too, because I was also going to Hawaii. Brent and Kyle sacrifice so much for other people. If giving up some of my freedom for five months meant they could go to Kona, it would be worth it. They're doing good things that make a difference to so many people.

As Kyle always says, "It takes a village." But that village doesn't just get the two of them across the finish, it also gets them and their families to the starting line.

CHAPTER 18

KONA OR BUST

BRENT AND KYLE

"I am in awe that we will have this opportunity and cannot wait to share it with my brother. This is the culmination of our dreams. Together."

- BRENT PEASE

When we got home from Raleigh, life suddenly became a seventeen-week, balls-to-the-wall everything. We needed to focus not only on the obvious job at hand, training like never, but also had to consider fundraising, organizing, logistics, planning, hotels, and flights. Once we crossed all those tasks off our to-do list, our time spent in Kona would be a 140.6-mile joy ride. Once again, through the efforts of the entire village, we succeeded.

I embarked on the most intense training I've ever done. I spent twelve to fifteen hours per week on the bike in preparation for what Kona would throw at us. While training for Raleigh, I did a lot more by myself than I normally do, so my regimen to prepare for Kona became a matter of balancing work, family, and everything else going on. There's a great social aspect to training with other people, and I often missed that by training solo as much as I needed to.

Most days, I rode up in the North Georgia Mountains. It is gorgeous up there, while at the same time extremely physically taxing. There were many moments when I didn't want to go through with it, and I really struggled at times. Despite the difficulty, I didn't miss a single training session. Showing up is always the hardest part, although setting the alarm or turning down that extra dessert or drink is not always easy. But we both set a goal and worked hard every day to achieve that goal. This isn't always easy, but it starts with a single step forward. Just like in NYC in 2015, we have always kept moving forward. Find your passion and run towards it, always.

KYLE

Brent finally took me up to the North Georgia Mountains that I had heard so much about. It's not exactly safe riding up there when your bike takes up most of one lane on a rural two-lane road, not to mention the entire support crew we had with us. So much beauty and so much fun to be able to take in with Brent. Being a part of this process, and not just as an onlooker, has been one of the best parts of this journey. I sure hope to find my way back up to those mountains soon. It allowed me a chance to reflect, a chance to enjoy my brother, and a chance to train like I was racing in Kona.

BRENT

In addition to the intense training, I needed to concentrate on my nutrition. Immediately following Raleigh, Kyle and I shared a celebratory champagne toast, and I had a beer with a roast beef au jus sandwich and a dessert. That next day, I went cold turkey. No beer. No dessert. When I was at the peak of "training" before my first IRONMAN, I'd have five or six drinks with a hamburger or wings as my go-to meal during my unhealthy day. For Louisville in 2010, I really tried to change and lead the life that I saw for myself. So, symbolically, even if I am healthier in mind, body, and spirit than ten years ago, I always give up some of those guilty pleasures in training. I give up some of the things that remind me of where I was and how far I have come. But this wasn't 2007, or even 2010, and this version of Brent is a lot more dedicated than the old model.

My nutrition was on-point for Kona. Kyle and I were absolutely committed to it. I could not believe how much food I needed to eat in order to sustain this rigorous training regimen. I'd wake up at five in the morning and eat around seven with the kids, Then, I'd eat at ten and again at one or two in the afternoon. I'd train some more, eat at four or five before the kids got home, and then sit down for a full dinner with the family, washed down with a shake shortly thereafter. I'd often wake up at two in the morning with a craving for a post-midnight snack like a yogurt before starting the cycle again three hours later. I just couldn't keep up with the calories I was burning while training.

In order to train for more hours than my typical regimen included, which I had to do to get ready for Kona, we needed all the help we always talk about. Dani Grabol is an endurance legend. She holds records for biking across the country (yes, the entire country). She has finished many races that most people have never even heard of. She offered to help put together the logistics of this race and allow us to focus on the tasks at hand. She knew exactly what we would want and need when taking on a big endurance challenge. She was an amazing asset to our village and made so much of the planning seamless. Training for Kona meant doing something every day, totaling twenty to twenty-five hours of training a week. Sometimes I'd train alone, but many times I trained with Kyle. We peaked at a seven-and-a-half-hour bike ride together. We ran for miles upon miles. We flipped his boat to see how we would both respond. We didn't want to leave out anything and wanted to control everything we could.

The training was tough on Kyle. Even getting on the bike can be stressful for him because of the awkward position in which he is forced to sit. Between IRONMAN Wisconsin and Boulder, we kept refining the bike, both in order to make it more comfortable for him and to enhance our performance by making it more aerodynamic. From New Orleans to Raleigh, we made several additional small improvements. Prior to Kona, we scrapped everything we had created, went back to Curtis, our incredible bike mechanic, and built a spaceship befitting of Kona.

So, after spending six years helping Kyle adjust to the rigors of an eight or nine-hour bike ride, we asked him to learn how to manage a new bike in just seventeen weeks. This was no small task for any athlete, let alone Kyle with his many physical challenges. Curtis is a maestro, though, and spent many long nights at his shop tinkering away on our bike. Together with a new friend Dave Hardy, a manufacturer and race car mechanic, they took nearly thirty-five pounds off our bike and lowered Kyle's profile significantly. We were always thinking about the wind and how to maintain our position with Kyle on the front of the bike.

We took stock of everything on that bike. After building a new seat befitting of a NASCAR race car, we looked at the angles of the seating and my aero position behind Kyle, the wheels, the pedals and even the bottle cages. Finishing was the only option.

What we ended up with was truly an engineering marvel. When you look at NASCAR teams, they need support at every level. So much of what we do is just like that, right down to slapping logos on everything. Hey, we need those sponsors too.

Truly what Curtis built was a special machine. It was almost space like and best of all? Kyle would ride in front, the captain of our ship that was put together in under 17 weeks. For a normal bike build that might seem a bit long. But we were taking the combined weight and efforts of two humans and trying to get them through one of the toughest 112-mile bike courses on the circuit.

On our longest ride, during an excruciatingly hot day in August, we made our final "test" run of the new bike. It was one of the hottest days of the year, and we needed to be out in the elements for most of the day. It was just a few of us out there for this long endurance test before the race. We brought Wright Mitchell, a close friend and supporter, along with Ian Evans, who helps Kyle in his daily life, along with supporting KPF at our larger events. We all love to bike, so we figured why not enjoy this challenge together.

Every training session, every occasion that summer, brought out some of the best in our village; we appreciated days like this, and called on these positive memories often during the race. Kyle really struggled out there on that ride, though. It was hard for him to eat in his new position, his hydration system was not working like we wanted it to, and, well...it was damn hot outside. We had to visit all the sag stops to get him extra calories, get him more fluids, and reapply sunscreen. It was just a brutal day for all of us, but especially for Kyle.

I asked him afterwards how he felt, and he said, "Oh, well, my neck hurts." I was irritated with him and said, "Well, Buddy, we gotta figure this out." And he said, "It always hurts." The more we talked about it, though, the more we both came to appreciate that anyone on the bike for seven-and-a-half hours would have some level of discomfort. We knew we could tinker a little more with his positioning and padding, but the reality was that he was going to need to be prepared for a dogfight on race day. The seven-and-a-half hours in the Georgia heat was as good a training day as he could possibly take on.

KYLE

That day in Cartersville was one of the more challenging days I've ever had in training. I had never trained like this before, nor had so much fun. Every week was a juggling act, and every weekend was a chance to do something more to get myself ready. I was so prepared, in fact, that when they flipped me in the boat, I just rolled myself over. Everyone's mouth dropped open and I was just thinking, *Yeah, if I am gonna race Kona, I might need to manage some of this, too.* The journey is always the best part. When we look back on this, the summer of 2018 is one that I shall always remember for the rewards I gained.

BRENT

I was hurting, too. I had been on the bike for seven-and-a-half hours as well, so it made sense that we hurt, but I was nervous because it was Kyle. We were all training hard. In one span, I was on the bike for twenty-eight hours over eight days. I did a three day mini-camp between Saturday and Monday on Labor Day weekend. Then, on Thursday, I rode for eight hours for good measure in the North Georgia Mountains, totaling 121 miles for the ride and nearly 500 miles in the week

We were about a month away from Kona when I called Matthew and said, "I want the race to be right now, Coach." I was trying to temper my enthusiasm because I was so physically ready. Unfortunately, my body started to break down shortly thereafter. That was my peak, so I had to start refining. The next few weeks before we really started resting were the most challenging for me. I was exhausted, both physically and emotionally. Erica needed me, I still had to raise money, and I still had work to do every day. For most of the summer, Erica would get up to go to the gym at five in the morning, and I would get up with her and work at the computer. I had two hours before the kids woke up to catch up on email. My friends would suggest that I take a break, but I still had to work on the foundation, and I had athletes to coach. That last three or four-week period was difficult. I just wanted to lay in bed, but we had so much we needed to do.

CHAPTER 19

MAHALO TO KAILUA KONA

BRENT

"What Brent and I accomplished this week is proof that you can do anything in life, as long as you give it your all."

- KYLE PEASE

After a surprisingly uneventful sixteen-hour flight from Atlanta to Los Angeles to Kona, we touched down at the Ellison Onizuka Kona International Airport. You could just feel the energy as we exited the plane. Everything that happened provided us with another special moment.

I woke up on Sunday, ordered a fresh pot of Kona coffee and just sat and stared at the endless Pacific Ocean. It was peaceful and quiet, but at the same time, powerful and energizing. I've done enough of these events with Kyle to know that something was going to smack us in the face on race day, and I wanted to bottle this sense of calm, to be able to draw upon it when we needed it.

On Monday morning, I went for a swim by myself and thought, *This is it. I've watched this on TV. I've read about it. Now, I'm really here. I'm swimming on the island swim course. I'm looking down and there are fish everywhere, swimming all around me.* Later on in the week, I took Kyle in the boat out on the course and stopped at the "Coffees of Hawaii" boat.

The sons of Dick Pease were doing the "touristy stuff" and laughing all the way out to the boat, imagining what our dad would be saying.

On Tuesday, we ran together, and the heat was extreme. The air was relatively calm, but we could still feel the running chair getting slowed by the Hawaiian winds. My heart rate was through the roof for the entire run, and I just kept wondering how the heck we were going to pull this off. The island was every bit as beautiful as we had read, but you must be there to experience the ruthlessness of racing there. Our short training sessions were, as you can imagine, eye-opening in many ways. The stunning beauty of the Hawaiian landscape vis-a-vis the homeliness of the angry winds and weather created an emotional tug of war between love and hate. I was starting to work myself into a frenzy. Kyle was the ever-present voice of reason, though, and here he was, just having a blast. He was with all his favorite training buddies. Betty's husband Ernie snapped photos of us with each of his five cameras. Betty screamed and yelped each time we passed, and why not? We were here, in the world championships!

Kyle

One of the best parts of the entire week were our short training sessions together. It usually meant a few of our friends would come out to join us. Sharing the energy and beauty of the island with people that had worked so hard to help get us here was a very special part of the week for me. If I ever find myself on that island again, I will be sure to soak up each moment just like that again.

BRENT

On Wednesday, we faced our first near-disaster. We decided to go for a bike ride, but when we went to take the bike off the rack, we encountered a huge problem. The bike was constructed with very special welds that allow the cables to run from the rear of the bike to the front wheel to help with steering. During transit, the weld had apparently snapped. Though I wasn't exactly panicking, I was starting to get nervous. Everybody jumped on their phones to come to our rescue and try to figure this out. Ian finally found a bike shop not too far away. As it turned out, the mechanic was an auto mechanic who had done work on handicapped vans before. Perhaps it was the right time and place, but this man was exactly who we needed. Curtis, the ever-calm mechanic, told us to go relax, and that he would be back.

He and Ian walked the bike the short distance up the hill, where the auto mechanic repaired our welds. Curtis enjoyed telling him all about the construction of the bike and about the two brothers who would ride this steed. Upon completion of the work, he wouldn't accept a single dime for payment. He simply wished us well and went back to repairing cars. Kyle always talks about each of us having a gift to share with the world. It is up to each of us to open that gift and share it. Kyle does that every day and inspires everyone he meets. Meeting people willing to share much of themselves, in turn, provides us with equal inspiration and drives us in all we do.

We continued our ride and I educated Kyle about the course, pointing out trees and how they reacted to the winds. He really got the chance to experience it all and to be the copilot. He understood that at times during the race, I might be grinding so hard on the pedals that he would need to manage every other detail. This doesn't work without Kyle, and it doesn't work without me—a team in the truest sense possible.

The check-in took place on Friday, and was one of the cooler things we experienced all week. Everyone was there and it was an absolute spectacle. As we came walking in, we heard the announcer say, "Here are the Pease Brothers from Atlanta," and everybody gave us a rousing ovation. And this was the day before the race. When we'd competed before, like in Boulder or Madison, no one was even there the day before the race. At Florida, they yelled at us to move our car because we were illegally parked. In Kona, we received a hero's welcome while we put our bike in the transition area.

Despite having been a fan of IRONMAN for nearly a decade, to finally be in a place that is so sacred to the sport was mind-blowing. The mass swim start in Kailua Bay or biking through the lava fields were experiences we had witnessed on TV, but that did not do them justice. The trade winds blow while you're pedaling down the Queen Ka'ahumanu Highway, and it's hot as hell. The temperatures are typically between eighty-four and ninety degrees at that time of year, but it never cools off. At night, it's seventy-eight to eighty degrees, and the lava rock heats everything.

One of the highlights was our Thursday morning interview on *Breakfast with Bob*. Bob Babbitt is considered a legend at Kona, despite, as he boasts, "being incredibly slow at swimming, cycling and running." Bob is a member of the IRONMAN Hall of Fame and the USA Triathlon Hall of Fame, cofounder of *Competitor Magazine* and the Challenged Athletes Foundation. He also created *Competitor Radio* and the Muddy Buddy Ride and Run series. Here Kyle and I were, sitting with Bob Babbitt, and we were as cool as the other side of the pillow, making fun of each other on world-wide Kona TV. At the same time, we held each other's hands and kept telling each other, "We're going to do this thing."

Bob absolutely loved Kyle. He knows our history. Dick and Rick Hoyt were the last team to finish Kona in 1999, and for years, duo teams have come out and tried to replicate their feat. None of them have finished. Bob was trying not to make it obvious, but he told us about it and was nearly saying, "Hey guys. A lot of people have tried this and failed. I'm not sure you are going to be any different." History would go on to show that, through hard work, love, dedication, and God's good graces, our results proved to be different. Later in the week, Bob named our interview as one of his top ten of the seventy-five interviews that he filmed during the week. That in itself would not overshadow the results of the race, but it was still a pretty nice aside to the main event.

Erica said that I'm usually calm on race day, but in reality, it's like ducks on a pond. Everything looks good on the surface, but you can't see what's really going on underneath. I was wound up like a top. I often am on race day, and my dad usually gets the brunt of it. On our way to the start, Kyle stopped for a prayer, which I initially didn't realize until I turned around and no one was there. I started walking really fast, getting anxious. I was trying to be patient, but inside, I was thinking, *Let's go, let's go, let's go.*

I turned the corner and saw the start line; rather than being excited, I was getting testy. Kyle and I got to transition with Greg and Jason (Dani's husband), who had become part of our crew at Boulder. We were only allowed two on the Kona crew, so we chose Jason and Dad.

Dad has supported us from the beginning and loves being a part of this, but often tends to get caught up in the festivities, and isn't always as available as we need him to be. We reminded Dad that as part of our two-person crew, we would need him to be near transitions, and that he wouldn't be able to come out on the course like he had in Florida. We couldn't say, "Oh, well, Richard's not here, bring someone else in."

Jason was the perfect guy to support us while also keeping Dad reeled in. At Boulder, Jason had taken control of the situation, commanding us: "Take this salt. Drink this water. Sit there until you're ready. Just be calm." He was like that with Dad as well: "Richard, shut up. Richard, take care of Kyle."

Greg got into the starting area because he was helping another wheelchair athlete, but had been given permission to help the other physically challenged athletes when he wasn't actively occupied. Greg helped us initially build the foundation and wrote one of the first generous checks we ever received. His daughter, Marin, was also the second athlete we supported. It worked out perfectly that Greg was able to assist us a bit as well; since I swam faster than his athlete, he helped us out of the water and got us ready for the road.

Just before the swim, Kyle and I finally got to enjoy a moment together. It always seems to happen like this. The chaos of race week finally subsides once we find ourselves in the water, with the race about to start, and we're back to being just two brothers. Together. Before the cannon went off, I looked at Kyle and told him, "Being your brother has been one of the greatest pleasures of my life. I am going to give you my all today and ask that you do the same." Not that I had a doubt, but he promised me he would. These thoughts consumed me throughout the day. I would not allow the negative emotions to win, and if they did creep in there, my brother would surely pull me through it, just as he has done many times before. I was so honored to be out there with this incredible human and share the incredible opportunity we had in front of us.

Once the cannon went off, there was no drama. I couldn't believe how fast I swam. I always pull energy from my family or Kyle. Every day, when Caroline comes home, she bangs on the door. I open it and she came running in and says, "That's my daddy," and she hugs me. I kept that image on replay in my mind to inspire me throughout the day.

Though I normally don't time my swim, I checked my watch. We had started at roughly 7:20, and it was now 8:27. I initially thought that my watch malfunctioned. I looked at Dani and screamed, "I swam in an hour and seven? Are you f-in kidding me?" Everyone in earshot heard me. I was in disbelief that, in an ocean and without a wetsuit, we were nearly fifteen minutes faster than we'd anticipated. I looked over at our fans, pumped my fist, and took off on the bike.

A crazy fall day with the Pease boys.

The annual Turkey Day Game. Brent and I are in the
huddle while Dad and Evan plot their defense.

A typical family photo complete with a strong selection in headwear.

Evan was the real musical talent, but we tried to join in.

Fall Catalogue option 1. Just me and the bros in a chair in the middle of a field.

An early tri for us. I was clearly having some fun! I still do when I'm out there with everyone.

Getting ready with our favorite crew member, Dad.

The first KPeasey bike. More than 400 pounds of human and steel.

On the Queen K with Brent aboard KONA1!

Woah, Nellie!

Prepping for IRONMAN Boulder in 2017.
Equipment was much improved by then.

IMFL 2014.

Our first IRONMAN together in 2013.
One of the most amazing days of my life.

Beth's son Josh running alongside us up Old Saulk Pass in Madison, Wisconsin, in 2013.

Finishing the bike in Kona. I was ready to get off!

Coming out of the water.

Posing with the first athlete we ever shared the course with, Jake Vinson.

Racing in our first tri of 2011, St Anthony's Oly triathlon.

Leading a race with Brent. We like to go fast!

I was a good looking young man. Plus, I clearly had my sights on Hawaii from an early age.

Brent jokes that we both sat on the sidelines together.

Brent with his wife Erica.

Right after the Kona bid, Brent was welcomed home by his children Caroline and Henry.

Finishing the swim of our first tri in 2011.

Me and my bud, Noah.

Everything has come a long way. Even the boat! Finishing up in 2011.

KYLE

R ace morning, I was a ball of nerves. I tried eating, but everything just barely slid down my throat. I tried going to the bathroom and was just too nervous. Talking? Out of the question. As we neared the start area, Greg pulled me and a few others aside, and we said our prayers together. A new calm came over me, and I frantically began looking for Brent. I have seen him enough on race morning to know where his mind was likely heading. Once in transition, we both watched the sunrise and watched the pro race begin to take shape. I closed my eyes and harnessed the energy of this island. As we loaded into the boat, a wave came upon us and crashed right over the boat and all over me. So much for keeping me dry before the bike. I started to laugh and yelped at the onlookers. Before I knew it, Brent grabbed the boat and started getting past the crashing waves to the swim start area. Those moments together before the race were the true calm before the storm...

BRENT

W hen biking, cadence is the speed at which you pedal, and relates to your bike's speed. Riding in a low gear will offer very little resistance, but it will take furious pedaling to go fast. Riding in a high gear will make the pedals harder to push but won't require as many revolutions to attain a high speed. Pedaling furiously in a low gear is called spinning, while pedaling slower in a high gear is called mashing.

I had been given strict instructions not to mash the pedals on the new version of the bike. It was so perfectly built by Curtis and all the guys at Cannon Cyclery. Our supporters ran along the seawall to watch us as we cruised by, and it was intense. My original training buddy, Steve, popped up on the road, swinging his fists and screaming so loud that it was hard for me refrain from mashing the pedals to show everybody just how strong we were. We were flying up the hill on mile 0.4, with a mere 111.6 miles ahead of us.

Kona is such a big race that they limit where spectators can be along the course. In Boulder, there were long stretches of road where there were dozens of people cheering for us. In Panama City, people were driving all over the highway to catch up to us, to the point that I thought Dad was going to get killed passing bikers on a double-line on Highway 79. In Wisconsin, supporters were everywhere. We never had to ride far before we went by someone we knew who was waiting to cheer us on. I knew in Kona we were going to have to be prepared to cheer ourselves on during many long, brutal stretches where spectators weren't allowed. Riding twelve miles per hour for thirty to thirty-five miles meant riding about three hours by ourselves, and that's a mental grind. In the week leading up to the race, we talked about how there could be beauty, pain, and suffering all in one place. There we were, biking through these gorgeous lava fields, just Kyle and me in the world championship, but there was no one there and nothing else around us but miles of pahoehoe and a lava rock.

For the first thirty to thirty-five miles that it's for you, then you turn around Kawaihae and the real fun begins. You begin working your way towards Hawi (ha-vee), which includes a nearly nineteen-mile steady upwards climb to the turn around. After that tedious stretch, we dropped down in elevation before another long climb back up. We entered town around mile forty with another nineteen to go before the turn-around return trip. The last six of those miles were brutal, but we got a boost of energy when we saw people at the turn. The winds were pretty good all day, maybe eight to ten miles per hour overall, nothing like what we'd had in Florida, but that nineteen-mile stretch was the one time we struggled with them.

Anything that's not a tailwind impacts us. The way our 10.5-foot bike frame was designed was best suited for a headwind or tailwind, but we had to deal primarily with crosswinds. I could feel the impact on our ride; I tried to pedal through it, but I could feel frustration from Kyle. Despite the winds, it was all relative. In Wisconsin, when we started going up the hills, we were averaging three or four miles per hour. In Kona, we were doubling that speed. Part of that was our fitness level, and part was the performance of the bike. I said, "Buddy, I'm doing everything I can." He asked for some food, and I asked if he could just wait until we muscled through this difficult stretch of road. He begrudgingly agreed.

When we got to the turn-around in Hawi, we were worried that if we didn't make an adjustment, his ankles were going to get torn up by the bike frame. We fixed his feet, grabbed some food and we were off again. We had a cut off to make.

At that point, we started to fly. Suddenly, the six to eight miles per hour we did climbing up to the little town of Hawi was now twenty-six, then twenty-eight, and eventually thirty-four miles per hour. We were motoring and making up some of that lost time. At certain points during the descent, I told Kyle to just look around, as we were surrounded by clear blue ocean and breathtaking views for miles. The cuts on his ankles might not seem so bad if he was able to focus on the surrounding beauty. As we turned to make the short and steepest climb up to Kawaihae, we really watched our cadence. As we passed Matthew and Steve, we got a quick check on the college football scores of the day. Just like in Wisconsin, or our living room growing up, we needed to catch up on sports to feel like our world was in balance.

KYLE

We had driven up to Hawi to check the climbs and the turnaround on Sunday, the day after we arrived. We talked about the wind and this stretch of road. I was ready for it and knew Brent would be, too. Come race day, I was laying at nearly a forty-five-degree angle to stay out of the wind. Being directly in the sun meant I needed to wear BIG frame sunglasses, sun sleeves on my arms and legs, and enough sunscreen for a family of five. None of it made a difference. I was burning up, struggling to eat, and my ankles had slipped off my foot plates and were being torn apart by the shiny aluminum. That was, without a doubt, the hardest part of the ride. We were averaging six miles per hour and just watching the race pass us by, waiting for the wind to be at our back. All I wanted to do was hit the turnaround so we could descend.

As we made our adjustments and grabbed more food, I finally had a chance to see what we had just done, the miles of ocean and lava rock and low trees lightly swaying in the breeze. It was hard not to smile. I looked at Brent. He nodded in agreement and gave me a big grin right back. World champs, Buddy! Let's go!

BRENT

As we hit the short but incredibly brutal climb, we kept returning to the little engine that could. Our favorite mantra for climbing on the bike is, "I think I can, I think I can…" It may seem juvenile, but it is a perfect source of motivation for us whenever the going gets tough. And, after all, who is more juvenile than we are? Matthew had this matrix he built for us prior to the race. It gave us an idea of where we needed to be at each mile marker on the high or low side. Going up to Hawi, we'd started creeping towards the low side—as in we risked not getting to the cutoff in time. During the nineteen miles to Hawi, we had continually lost ground, and we were really starting to doubt our ability to pull this off. As we made the turn back onto the Queen K, however, we were nearly forty-five minutes ahead of schedule, thanks to some fast descents. I told Kyle, "We got this." He reminded me that despite the feelings of confidence, we had to remain focused! We had to stay on task and cover these last thirty-two miles together. We said, "Let's leave the hard climb to Hawi in the rearview mirror, and let's focus on enjoying the end of this ride!"

The one thing I hadn't thought about is how we always have the support of each other on the bike. We rarely have these deep meaningful conversations on the bike, but when I got into a dark place during the ride, I would dig down and ask Kyle things we don't usually discuss. I figured taking my mind off the ride and listening to his responses would help lessen the physical pain. At one point, I said, "Tell me why you love me." Kyle didn't even hesitate and responded, "Because you are the man. Do you see where we are—where you brought me? Let's do this, man. I love you." I choked back tears, thinking about his spontaneous response, and thought for a minute about why he was thankful for me to allow him to have this experience, while I was equally dependent on and thankful for him. Without him, I might still find a way to finish, but with him, I wouldn't allow myself to fail.

He then asked me, "Tell me why you love Erica." I responded just as automatically, "Because she helped make this possible. Because she brought me two beautiful kids. Because she lets me be me."

These were the conversations we got to have during all the pain and suffering we were both experiencing. I was struggling to push through the pain of the ride, and Kyle's ankle was getting torn up. He was having trouble eating because of the way he was lying down. He was getting dehydrated and tired. We were both physically and emotionally spent as we approached the final long climb of the day, and needed each other to provide us with a diversion to get through it all. Deep discussions like these usually happen when we have some downtime together, lying in our beds in a strange hotel room in the middle of the night, but it was powerful for both of us to have them during that nineteen-mile stretch. I couldn't have biked nearly as fast as we did if I was alone, and that's as fast as I've ever moved on a bike with Kyle.

We both rode silently for a few miles, thinking of the responses to both questions. Though not saying a word, we contemplated. We felt warm inside. We felt stronger and more together than we had been moments before. Together, we had experienced a moment powerful enough to carry us through the next difficult portion of the course. Together, we wheel.

We got to the climb, and I kept telling myself, "Don't mash the pedals." As we were going up, Matthew was there and I thought about the matrix to determine what kind of shape we were actually in. Erica was there, too, and told us, "We're not going to see you until transition, but there are some people waiting ahead in Waikoloa." That was helpful to know because there were still thirty-two miles after the turn and that was a long way to go without anyone to look forward to.

I looked at my watch, did the math, and realized we could average just ten miles per hour the rest of the way and still make the cutoff. I excitedly told Kyle, "We've got it, Buddy. I just did the calculations and we have this in our back pocket." He yelled at me with anger in his voice, and like a good copilot, told me to focus. I reeled myself in and said, "You're absolutely right. Let's do everything we can for the final thirty-two miles. Let's eat. Let's drink. Let's focus." In that final thirty-two miles we both remained intent on reaching the goal. After nearly getting ahead of ourselves, we focused on each movement and, with near anger in his voice, Kyle kept repeating to me to FOCUS as we moved forward!

This was the most intense race we have ever been in. Both our physical and mental states were at world championship level, and I would go back and do it all again in a heartbeat. I've seen Kyle compete in a lot of ways before, but never like this. He was in the zone, competing fiercely, driving me to the finish line. Kyle borrows my legs and I borrow his spirit, and this had never been truer than it was that day.

There was one stretch around mile one-hundred when I was just trying to get to the airport. The airport was at mile 105, and from there, we'd have just seven miles to go. In Florida, Kyle counted every mile for me for fifty miles. So for that five mile stretch in Kona, that's what I asked him to do. Mentally, you need to have a lot of tools at your disposal to be successful at IRONMAN. Kyle's toolbox is built from a lifetime of struggling, and he keeps each of these tools razor sharp, hard as steel, and readily at his disposal. At that moment, I took something he had taught me during our IRONMAN in Florida, and now shared it with him. Looking back on it now, it was exciting that I was able to do that.

Once we got past the airport, it was hard not to get excited. We were back among all our friends, and we saw Betty running her marathon on the other side of the Queen K. As soon as we got into transition, I was anticipating the drama that we had come to expect. In Wisconsin, there was drama as we made it to transition just two minutes before the cutoff. In Florida, there was the drama associated with wondering if we would even have the strength to make it to the transition. In Boulder, it was the same thing, as we were falling apart on the bike due to the conditions, the altitude, and the mistakes we made with our nutrition.

In Kona, we rolled into transition and experienced a soothing calm. "We could sit here for an hour," I told Kyle. "We're fifty-one minutes under the cutoff." There was no drama, and it was almost an equally unsettling feeling, but in reverse. I was about to throw my arms up to flex for Kyle, before realizing they had whisked him off and were dressing him in a separate area. The pier in Kona is really small. Getting 2,500 bikes on there is a feat, let alone a ten-foot-long contraption like ours.

When we were all changed and back together, I looked at Kyle and said, "Hey, look. We can have a PR and can really smash this thing." We wanted to make a statement and say, "Look, we deserve to be here. We deserved to be here five years ago. We deserve this opportunity."

We also just wanted to have a good day and just enjoy being here. I looked at Kyle, knowing how tired he was, and asked, "Are you ready?" He looked at me with fire in his eyes and said, "Let's do this." We were off with plans to enjoy our 26.2-mile victory lap.

I regret that we didn't spend a little more time in T2, because on the run during every other IRONMAN, there was never a doubt in my mind that we would finish. We knew that once we got to the bike cutoff, we were good. During this run, I began to have some self-doubt. I realize in retrospect that I was a touch dehydrated, enough so that it manifested in the form of diarrhea. Obviously, diarrhea is a very funny topic, not to mention the abundant flatulence that goes along it. Once again, physically and emotionally, it fueled us during the early part of the run.

We had barely made it to mile two when I informed Kyle. "I'm in some serious pain, Bud. I need to find a Porta Potty." We've learned from all these races how to manage things like this. I stuck Kyle with a volunteer, who fed him while I started dry-heaving in the bathroom, before destroying this poor Porta Potty while trying to restart my body. I exited what had once been a Porta Potty with beads of sweat pouring down my forehead. We got going again and I was fine for five more miles, but I still didn't feel right.

They had traffic cones about five feet apart, splitting the course, and the best I could do was to will myself to make it from one cone to the next. If I hadn't gotten into that mental space, I would have stopped and walked. Had we walked, we would have come in by midnight, and it would have been dramatic, but we wanted to prove that we belonged here, so walking wasn't an option. We had a bit of a chip on our shoulders, so running across the line with ample time to spare was the desired method of finish.

Next came our run up Palani Drive. I'd had it in my mind that, no matter what, I was going to run up that hill. I felt like that was a statement. To run up the hill on the toughest part of the course, at a time in the race when a lot of people were walking, would be another example of proving to the critics that we belonged. I had pumped myself up all week and was going to attack the hill. I charged right up it.

KYLE

Palani is that iconic part of the run course. It can make or break many a marathon right there. Charging up it on the bike in the early part of the race and again on the early part of the run felt like a statement. Like coming out after the kickoff and running a deep post route smack at the safety. We both wanted it, and charging up that hill with Brent was an all-timer. I still get chills at the sounds of the crowd as we moved with authority up that hill.

BRENT

Coming back down later, we had to be more careful. Usually when Kyle and I do a race and we're going down, I just go. The chair and his weight want to go one direction, and that is down. We knew that this was a very dangerous part of the course, however, and we had to hold back a bit.

At mile seven, the dehydration returned. At that point, I stopped even taking in calories, because everything was going right through me like poop through a goose—coming in the mouth and then going right back out the front or right through the back.

At one point, we were running in total darkness. I could see enough to run, but nothing more. Kyle asked, "Where are the lights?" I told him, "Dude, it costs so much money to run the utilities on the island that they have just enough lights for emergencies." These are the conversations we had to keep us going through the dark.

I was starting to move again, but at mile ten or eleven, I made a return trip to the Porta Potty. I was light-headed and dizzy, worried that I might pass out and fall down on the side of the road. There was even fear that our journey would end with me passed out in the Porta Potty. Though laughable now, being found face first in the crapper was not the way Kyle and I wanted to be remembered. Kyle could see and hear what was going on and offered his support, though there wasn't much either he or I would be able to do about it.

About halfway through the course, we turned left off the Queen K and onto the area known as the Natural Energy Lab, which everybody always talks about as being the hardest part of the course. It's where the island produces a lot of its energy, and there's nothing back there. It's a desolate place, with huge pipelines that pump cold water up from the ocean to be studied, and huge solar panels that gather energy from the sun to fuel the island. It comes at that point in a 140-mile race where you start to have self-doubt. The temperature dropped, and it was dark and eerie for about a three-mile stretch. Those who are weak of mind are likely going to struggle during this stretch, and yet it would be a horrible place to crash and burn.

Kyle was all wet; he'd been sweating. This chill in the air made him cold, and he started shivering. We had nothing for him, as it hadn't been getting cold at night all week. Then the rain started, and it came down in buckets—harder than either of us had ever experienced before. I hadn't eaten, the light was dampened by the rain, and we couldn't see a thing at this point. Maybe this was our drama.

We'd been racing for 120-odd miles, and still had about fourteen or so to go. It was crazy. Around mile fifteen or sixteen, I left Kyle with a volunteer, went into my last Porta Potty, and exploded again. Expulsed. Everything. I came out of there and I said, "Buddy, we've got to figure this out. I don't know what to do." He told me, "Let's get a little something to eat. Let's figure it out."

At the next station, they had chicken broth, and I took a few sips. It was really hot and it revived me. The sodium, just getting something that my stomach could hold, brought me back to life. One of the volunteers gave Kyle some towels and we were moving again. As we came around the bend from the Energy Lab, there were all our friends on bikes, our own group of cheerleaders, talking us through it and cheering us on.

At the beginning, I could only run five feet at a time. Then, I could see traffic lights, three-quarters of a mile to a mile apart. I was able to run a further distance without stopping. Matthew was out there saying, "Just get to the next traffic light." I was getting calories in again, feeling better, and we were really moving. I could feel the burn in my legs. I almost enjoy that physical response when I've been struggling, then finally start to feel life in my muscles again.

That was just past mile twenty-four—nothing was going to stop us.

We could have crawled the rest of the way to the finish and still made it. Once we got back onto Ali'i Drive, everything that makes the island magical was right there—the people, the music, everything. Matthew caught us one more time and said, "Enjoy this."

I think I slowed down, though Kyle says we were flying. We ran into the loudest, most unbelievable reception that I've ever heard. I started to tear up a little bit. There's that initial finish photo where I think you can see a tear, but it immediately evaporated. When Rick and Dick did Kona in 1989, they finished on a flat road into a tape. When they finished in 1999, it was already becoming a spectacle. In 2018, it was like the Super Bowl and the Packers in 1966. They don't even have any film footage of that, but Kona has that giant feel. It was organic, a bunch of tough dudes and women who said, "Let's just see who can do the most. Let's see who can suffer more than anyone." And it still has that element.

Kyle and I suffered together, solo. We were out there, battling the elements with the best athletes in the world, with everybody. Some finish lines we've shared with everyone, like in Wisconsin, where I hugged Erica and high-fived a bunch of people, but this was the one finish line I wanted to just share with Kyle. There would be other opportunities to celebrate with everybody.

We approached the finish line, running through the chute and up the ramp. I came up to the top and stopped. It was just us, but the crowd was just deafening. I talk about how I want to make Kyle an athlete and how I want Kyle to have this as his own crowning moment. Kyle makes me an athlete. How else would I have been able to compete in the world championships? Certainly not by myself. Kyle brought me to the world championships. He elevated me to make me a world championship athlete. I looked over at Kyle and he was screaming. His helmet was over his eyes. I could feel the energy.

I looked over and saw Erica jumping up and down—this woman who had lived with me in a basement in her parents' house in order to help make my dream, our dream, come true. Though not wearing a number pinned to her chest, Erica had, in many ways, struggled and sacrificed just as much as Kyle and I had. She had symbolically swum each stroke and pedaled each mile on the bike. Erica had run each mile through the Energy Lab. Without her, without Kyle, I may be an IRONMAN, but I am not a world champion. Without them, it's equally likely that I'm an overweight drunk still trying to figure it all out.

I turned and looked at Kyle and started shaking his face. The next thing I know, my feet were in the air, and I was jumping up and down. It got louder and louder with every jump. Then I stopped and turned, and our families were there, and we were hugging. There were pictures, and then I started to realize what I had done, and I just collapsed. Erica picked me up.

They pushed us through to the athlete holding area, where it was eerily silent. There have been many moments when I wanted to go back through that athlete exit and feel it again, share it all with Kyle once more. I hope he feels the same. This time, we got everything out of that moment that we possibly could. That was for me and Kyle. When we finished, it was for everybody. In that one hundred yards to the finish, it was just me and him, climbing up to the top of the mountain. It has been a long slope.

But then, that's what all of this has been about. That's what Charles Harris was all about. That's what this has always been about for us. There have been other things for us as a foundation, and even more as a family, but there are these special few moments that I get to share with Kyle. How many siblings do we know who talk about how they have slowly drifted apart over the years? Kyle and I have been able to share so much together. These two moments are always going to stick with me, when all the outside noise has stopped for a second. That last one hundred feet, that moment at the top of the ramp when it was just the two of us. Those were the most powerful parts of the day for me, and the ones I'll hang on to for as long as I can.

CHAPTER 20

Beyond the Finish

Kyle

Never in my wildest dreams,
Though believing that I can.
Did I think I'd hear the announcer say,
"Kyle Pease, you're an IRONMAN."

- Where There's a Wheel, There's a Way

Those are the heartfelt words that begin our first children's book. That stanza rings so true whenever I try to make sense of the incredible ride that Brent and I have been on and continue to cruise on. Each time I hear the announcer utter those words, I get a lump in my throat and butterflies in the pit of my stomach. For those who don't believe that dreams can come true as the result of perseverance, hard work and dedication, I ask that you look at my life one more time. On paper, none of my accomplishments would seem to be possible, but the world doesn't play out on paper. My achievements are the result of my indomitable spirit and tremendous amount of heart. Where I may have been robbed of many physical abilities, I was blessed with a surplus of both spirit and heart. That overabundance is what allows me to turn dreams into reality.

When others say that something is impossible, I encourage them to say and honestly believe the phrase, "Yes, you can, yes, we can, and yes, I can." Growing up, my mom used to remind me that we each have a special gift, and that it's up to each of us to open that gift and to share it. I hope, in sharing some of my experiences and strong beliefs, that I have been able to share some of my gifts with those who come to learn of our story.

This has been, and continues to be, a long journey for me. I cannot count the number of times I'd lie awake as a child, wondering what it might be like to get myself out of bed under my own power. What it might feel like to hit the game-winning homerun, or to catch a touchdown pass from my idol, Matt Ryan. I've longed to know the freedom of brushing my own teeth, feeding myself a meal, or running across the road to hug a friend. But, now I know. I am lucky and proud to be able to tell anyone who cares to hear my words that I am an IRONMAN World Champion athlete. Few who dot the planet can claim such a title, and I am one of those elite who have earned it. Each fall, the fittest people from around the globe converge on the sleepy little fishing town of Kona, Hawaii to test their endurance. To see if they have the muscle, the heart, the spirit, the unwillingness to give in. This is inarguably the hardest one-day endurance challenge on the planet. Those who survive it all within a predetermined period are dubbed Ironmen. Through an assist from my brother, but also through possessing all the ingredients needed to achieve such acclaim, I have been bestowed with the honor of such a title. Kyle Pease, IRONMAN World Champion athlete.

There are so many along the way who have helped to make this journey possible, and without their help and belief in me, I'd not have been able to experience or achieve any of this. As a village of sorts, they have helped mold me into the man that I am today. Each of you have had a hand in adding a small piece of encouragement, guidance, wisdom, strength or ability that has allowed me to proverbially rise out of my chair and become the version of me that stands before you today.

My parents may have played the biggest role, as they never accepted the word no and taught me to fight for what I believe in. They urged me to never give up, but they were there to cushion my fall each time I was unable to succeed. I cannot imagine what my life would look like without them as my true north.

My brothers carried me up mountains, swam with me in the pool, and pulled me on bicycles in the physical sense, but did the same with me spiritually and emotionally. They always included me in their adventures and helped me find the joy, no matter what my vantage point may have been. It is asking a lot to include your sibling in everything you do and everywhere you go even when they are able-bodied and do not alter your own experience through their attendance. When your brother is disabled, and his inclusion in every adventure represents a personal sacrifice for you, it is nothing short of heroic.

My teachers, aides, friends, and so many more that always accepted me for me, and never asked me to be anything other than me: You became the many individual spoons that stirred my pot. I was provided with the recipe for a life filled with happiness and success, and you provided me with the ingredients to make the stew.

Being chosen to compete in Kona in the fall of 2018 is an experience that I will never, ever never forget. It was truly the pinnacle of my life. When I came across the finish line, hand in hand with my brother, my body trembled. As the crowd rose to its feet, the hairs on the back of my neck stood at attention. I was about to become a world champion. To share that incredible experience with my brother is truly something I will always cherish, and it will stand out forever as one of the most unexpected, yet long-anticipated moments of my life.

Doctors would have scoffed had I told them my dream of becoming a world champion athlete. Understandably, doctors make their assessments based on physiological facts, and refrain from considering the will, the heart, and the desire of the human being. The odds of me becoming a world champion athlete were undoubtedly slight, but the only way they would have become impossible is if I had quit striving to achieve them. There were many times I questioned my will to continue, but I couldn't give up on a goal that had driven me for so long.

Evan sent Brent and me a text following our race in Kona that has allowed me to gain a full appreciation of what I will forever cherish about this journey:

The awards thing isn't what important here. I'm so proud of you guys. Accomplishing a dream is rare in life, and to witness you guys do that together was special for a lot of folks, especially me. Proud of your accomplishment. Even more proud to be your brother. Love you, dudes.

Accomplishing any dream in life is rare. My dream from my earliest years was to be an athlete. I appreciated being dressed like an umpire so my brothers could play baseball, but that wasn't my dream. I enjoyed participating by being wheeled around the bases under someone else's power, but that wasn't what I aspired to do. No, I wanted to experience what it felt like to be an athlete. In high school, I found a way onto the court as a team manager. In college, I majored in sports management to try and find a way into an arena that I loved. I never gave up, and worked hard to find a backdoor way into experiencing what it felt like to be an athlete. It wasn't until I crossed my first finish line that my life felt complete. I longed to feel that repeatedly, and became inspired by not only the destination, but by the incredible journey along the way.

EPILOGUE

KYLE

Betty pushed me towards my dream as we spent the day chatting in Louisville in 2010. She had me itching to give IRONMAN a try, and when Brent said yes when I asked a very simple question, the scratching of the itch began. When I am out there competing with other endurance athletes, I do not feel like I have a disability. I see what I am truly capable of and what my abilities are. I am not sure that I can fully convey that, inside my broken body, resides the heart of an athlete; just because I need Brent to propel me towards each finish line, doesn't make me any less of an athlete.

My final words of encouragement are to find your passion, find your dream, and chase it, because accomplishing a dream is rare. The journey was hard, but looking back, it was worth every painful moment. I would go back and ride a thousand more miles with Brent, just to talk, joke around, laugh and cry with my friend and brother.

So, what is next? I always felt like Kona would be the tipping point for The Kyle Pease Foundation and for people to witness what really drives me. The smiles at each finish line bring me a tremendous level of joy, seeing my hard work pay off. I hope that the platform of Kona gives us the opportunity to show everyone what is truly possible, and to give them the opportunity to find their finish line, too. I hope that we can show people what is beyond the finish line. That they can find their own paths to permanent change, and define themselves by what they can do, rather than by what they can't do.

There will be other races for Brent and me. We love this too much to accept our biggest race as our final race. When you achieve a goal, it is simply time to set a new one. I believe we will continue to race together for as long as we can carry each other through the day. Until the next occasion, we hope our story will inspire at least one other to chase their own dreams.

ACKNOWLEDGMENTS

BRENT

To Todd Civin: This book was not possible without your friendship, trust and careful guidance through this project. Neither of us understood how difficult writing a book would be, especially one where you are telling your own story. Thanks for all the interviews, the dinners, and even your travel to be with us and help bring this project together. You have put a tremendous amount of faith in us since 2012 and this project essentially began then.

Thank you to Kiley and the team at Mascot Books for working with us on such a special project. Your patience as we navigated this process, your guidance through it and your faith in the story was needed and greatly appreciated.

To the first board of KPF: You all worked tirelessly to help make this dream and vision a reality. We worked late into the night as volunteers and all took part in the physical work needed to make this thing work. We speak with great pride of that first board and all the energy invested from each of you. Amy Moore, John David Johnson, Chris Reilly, Sam Harrison, Michael Kidd, Chris Jones, Tim McTyre, Ben Spears, Jason Horrell, Jamie Sims, and our first legal expert Drew Marlar. Thank you all.

Greg: We started with wings and beer at a small sports bar in Atlanta and asked you to help us grow. You have done far more than that and have protected us like your own. You are an incredible friend and we cannot wait to see you and Marin find that next amazing finish.

Thank you to all the volunteers that have supported KPF, but especially my friend Mike Ragan. You have driven trucks around the country and made this feel like a family. One of the most special parts of KPF is our people, and you are our people.

We mention Matthew Rose time and again in this book but always as a coach. In 2010, I was truly seeking to make some changes in my life when I met you and the folks at Dynamo Multisport. One of Matthew's mentors focused on coaching the person and not just the sport. Well Matthew, you have coached the person and I thank you for the role you have played in helping me see the best version of myself beyond what I can do on a race course. Thank you for being our friend and mentor.

Betty: You can still make fun of me for that first time I sat on a bike next to you, but you have always given of yourself so willingly and worked so hard to help make all this a success. We could not have imagined racing without you in Kona. Truly a memorable experience.

To Dynamo Multisport and my many wonderful training partners over the years. Each of you helped those miles pass by, provided me guidance and friendship as I grew in this sport and as we built KPF. Thank you for many, many miles over the many, many years. Steve, Kathryn, Erin, Chris, Erik, Drew, Haley, Stacy, and many, many more.

To my FSU friends: My life changed when I got to FSU. I wouldn't change a thing and you have all helped support me through some of the best and worst in my life. Hearing from you all during the week of the race brought everything full circle and I cannot wait until we can ring in another national title together (in like ten or fifteen years).

To the Silvermans: Thanks for allowing me into your lives and ultimately into your basement. I appreciate your steadfast support when I roamed around your house in Lycra leaving you to wonder how I would ever make a life for your daughter. I always cherished our family dinners together and the conversations that would spring up from time to time. If the opportunity ever presents itself, I would be honored to call you roomies once again.

To Evan: You are a kind, caring, and compassionate brother. Thank you for allowing us to take this dream beyond three brothers racing and all the way to Kona, Hawaii. Growing up Peasey wasn't always perfect, but it was truly always perfect. Thanks for being such a strong figure in our family of five. I figure, it's time we grab a few shows together and come up with another heady playlist for NYE now that this journey has ended and before the next one begins. Evan, we've swung at each other, gotten in fights, hugged each other and shared our secrets with one another. Brothers all the way. I love you and we are all so proud of the man you are.

Mom and Dad: Thank you for teaching us what it means to never give up. What it means to take the word no and find a way to make that a positive yes. You have always encouraged us to chase our dreams and I hope you know we are as proud to call you Mom and Dad as you are to call us your sons. Our love to you. forever and always.

To Henry: One day you will look at me and never know a word of what happened the year you were born. I couldn't want or wish it any other way. But when you learn about your uncles, and you and your sister take your first swings, I hope you know just how deep the bond of family runs. Especially among siblings. You are a strong and powerful man and I hope that you learn the power of never giving up and the rewards that come from that. Love, your Dad.

To Caroline: I hope you know that my life was forever changed when I met you. I carried you with me through the Pacific, through the lava fields and down Ali'i Drive. I only hope you know that giving up is the easy thing. Powering through and staying true to your dreams is one of the hardest things I have done in my life. You are one of the greatest loves of my life and I am so proud to be your Dad.

Lastly, I would like to thank you, Erica. Without you none of this was possible. We lived in basements with children, we traveled to small towns with no names for vacations and we usually brought a bike. We never left our hometown and we always tried to include our families. This was as much for you as anyone. I love you.

Kyle

'd like to acknowledge Mom and Dad for helping me understand the definition of possible. For always supporting me and allowing me to roll through the waves and away from shore. I love you both and all you have given me.

To my care partners of past and present: Thank you for giving so selflessly of yourselves and allowing me to live in an independent life. It is each of you that make a bigger difference than you may ever fully understand.

Evan: We've shared a womb, a bedroom, basketball courts, and a deep bond that only twins will ever know. I am so proud to be your twin, so honored to be your brother. Love you, man!

Erica and Emily: I love you guys. Thank you for allowing me to take center stage time and again and supporting each wild dream!

To Coach Matthew, Greg, Dani, and Betty: Thank you for believing in us, thank you for helping bring us to start lines over and over.

Brent: Words cannot express my gratitude for helping me to become a world champion. You have been telling people since we finished that you had a front row seat to one of the greatest athletic achievements of your life. Well, I too witnessed something great and I am deeply thankful for that opportunity.

To the athletes of KPF: You have shown us so much love and shared so many miles with me. Figuratively and literally. I thank you for allowing me to be a part of your finish experience and look forward to our next great journey together! Together WE did!!